Shady Gardens

You can have as lovely a garden in the city as in the country.

Shady Gardens

How to Plan and Grow Them

EMILY SEABER PARCHER

PRENTICE-HALL, INC.   *New York*

Contents

Acknowledgments

NOBODY EVER WRITES a book alone. Certainly I haven't done so. All the people who have held out a helping gardening-hand or given me a plant have contributed to this one. Those I might have heard at a lecture, or whose articles I might have read have had a part in it. Many who have helped are forgotten, but my gratitude to them remains.

Probably I would never have begun this book if my father had not taught me to love nature and gardening, and wanted me to write. Probably I would never have finished it if it hadn't been for the patience and encouragement of my husband—and the publishers.

Mr. Arno Nehrling of the Massachusetts Horticultural Society has given me many a needed pat on the back for my lecturing and writing. I am grateful to the editorial staff of *Horticulture,* who were never too busy to help, and to Miss Manks and Mrs. Green in the library of the Horticultural Society.

Other helpful individuals were many: Mrs. Frances Williams, who knows about hostas; Mr. H. Gleason Mattoon, editor of the *Horticultural Newsletter;* the kind replies to my questionnaires from garden clubs; Mrs. Thomas Stafford; Miss Gloria Gould; Mrs. Forest Davidson; Marg and Al Berglund; and many friends in the Garden Club Federation of Massachusetts, who constantly give so much for the furtherance of gardening and its allied activities.

Through garden clubs, I gained the inspiration to find out more about gardening. Scientists may laugh, and business men scoff at such things as digging in the soil and replanting trees, but these activities have an inherent value that can be measured by no one. They are akin to religion, and are as indispensable. And so, to all those garden club workers, to zealots of conservation and the preservation of beauty spots, and to the unknown gardeners who might hold out a helping hand to other diggers and weeders, I give my deepest acknowledgments and thanks.

Emily Seaber Parcher

Introduction

✦✽✦✦✦✽✦✦✦✽✦✦✦✽✦✦✦✽✦✦✦✽✦✦✦✽✦✦✦✽✦✦✦✽✦✦✦✽✦✦✦✽✦✦✦✽✦

As I WRITE, spring is on the way. Down across the valley, through the White Pine boughs, I can see the Swamp Maples budding red against the blackish tree trunks on the rising woodland beyond. The White Oaks are losing last summer's leaves.

For weeks, the Dogwood buds have been close to bursting. The 8-foot Laburnum tree, that we moved last fall so skeptically, is glistening with silvery buds — proof that it weathered the winter successfully. The 3-foot Laburnum — sample of my first air layering, done two years ago — is thriving. Near it the Christmas-Rose is in bloom.

Sharon Station is gay with early Forsythia, but our bushes are later, and at that breath-taking point where myriads of buds are breaking. Tomorrow, or maybe the next day, the branches will be hung with golden bells. Spring will have arrived! The Flowering Quince is about to bloom too — everything almost two weeks early this year. Lilacs are showing prominent buds. Early Cherries are tipped pink or white.

The Crocuses the rabbits left have gone by. After weeks of bloom the Snowdrops are fading. So are the little golden cups of *Adonis amurensis* with their lacy green collars. Most

1

of the gardens have been uncovered, revealing Daffodil buds
fat with promise, Little *Puschkinias* wear gray-blue dresses,
like miniature Hyacinths, *Ajuga* and *Phlox stolonifera* are
beginning to look alive again.

Yesterday I removed some of the pine boughs in my shady
rock garden. Primulas are in bud, even the funny little
mounds of *P. denticulata*. *P. denticulata* var. *alba* is going to
bloom too; I was worried about it last summer. The Arbutus
has buds on it — under the few pine boughs I left over it.
I don't trust these late winter winds.

Here and there are stilettos of *Hosta* foliage. One Laurel
is very shrubby; perhaps there are a few rooted branches to dig
away and form new plants. The second Laurel in the shady
rock garden is rather spindling. The buds should have been
pinched off two years ago when I chopped it from its mother
bush. One of the Arborvitae is sad (red spider?); a second is
flourishing since I moved it from the hot terrace and gave it
plenty of compost. The Yew and Hemlock cuttings are turning into little bushes. Rosy sweet Violets are forming a carpet
behind one of the rocks. I dug one yesterday for a friend who
had given me two species of *Pulmonaria*.

When I refer to my shady rock garden, it is truly a garden in the shade. Four years ago, when we moved to Tree-
Tops, it was a rooty incline under oaks and aged pines,
between the edge of the upper garden and our shaded driveway. Most unfinished-looking, and I decided that when I
had all the other projects under control, I would do something about it.

But gardeners are impatient people! I started it the
second spring. There was no natural rock ledge, or even
many rocks, until we acquired half a load. Some of them were
fairly sizable. My husband and I rolled them end over end,

and ultimately they landed at their proper destinations. Distributed in groups of three and five, they make a fairly acceptable background for plants.

At first I thought I'd devote the shady rock garden entirely to *Hosta,* but that would have meant no contrast of foliage and no winter interest. Together with *Hosta* I settled on a group of favorite wild flowers, some evergreens, Phlox, Siberian Iris, and Tansy for summer color.

Although it receives almost no direct sunlight, the shady rock garden is light and airy. After two years, it is taking on the aspect of a cared-for place. Ivy has started to creep around some of the rocks. A baby Holly tree is at home and growing. The Arbutus has indicated it does not like late winter winds, and a patch has been moved to a more protected area.

When we moved here, one of the editors of *Horticulture* asked if I was still going to have shade to garden under. "I must," I replied. "After thirteen years of gardening in the shade at our other home, it is now so much a part of me that I couldn't be without it." And that is true. If I had to choose between rampant garden growth in the sun, but with no trees, and fewer blossoms because I had the trees, I'd choose the latter every time.

Trees are blamed because they are "dirty." Leaves, needles, cones, seed pods, catkins, have to be raked up from their shady carpets. Trees have roots that hump up a lawn, or sneak into a drain, or walk into a garden. Yet tree-roots, and the humus made from leaves, form our forest beds, and those forest beds are our water-sheds, with underground streams supplying water to communities hundreds of miles away. To me, a garden would not be a garden without trees, in spite of roots and seeds and shade. The backbone and background of my garden are the trees. This is the second garden that I have built from the leaves that have fallen from their branches. My soil is constantly being renewed and replenished from those leaves in the process of decomposition. Leaves and other organic materials make the soil live, and thus able to sustain the millions of plants seeking sustenance from it. Like the cycle of life — growth, death, decay and life again — my garden has its cycle too — soil, seed, tree, leaf, soil. Destroy one link and the chain is broken. Chemical nutrients might be added, but without the humus made from leaves, those nutrients could not be taken up by the fine root-hairs of the plants. Humus is a soil-builder, something that chemical fertilizers can never be.

If you have trees, and perhaps lament that you cannot maintain gardens under their branches, I say: "Be thankful for the blessings those trees offer you." You can raise flowers under them. You can have a garden in the shade. Not all things will bloom as well as in direct sunlight, but give them an abundance of humus, moisture, air, and room, and they will be very satisfactory. You will learn to love the trees, to enjoy the leafy shadows cast upon the earth beneath, to delight in white blossoms caught by a late afternoon sun under their branches, to know the fun of bringing out the shadows with yellows and pinks, and to appreciate the contrast in different kinds of foliage. You will have what others have not, and besides you'll have a garden, for in the pages to follow are some of the many things you can grow if you are to garden in the shade.

PART ONE

You Can Have Flowers in the Shade

1

Shade and Degrees of Shade

✣✣✣✣✣✣✣✣✣✣✣✣✣✣✣✣✣✣✣✣✣✣✣✣✣

PERHAPS YOU ARE one of those people who think that a garden should be riotous with the color and bloom of flowers. Flowers there must be, but a true garden has many objects of interest, numerous features arranged so that the result is an artistic achievement.

Garden-pictures can be made with a single tree, or a tree and a fence, or a tree with shrubs growing under it. Garden beauty can be built with terraces, with rocks and boulders, with pieces of driftwood, artistic old stumps, steps, terraces, grass, bird-baths, pools, and choice statues, as well as with plants and flowers. Even children's play equipment and other accessories should be considered when arranging a yard and garden. These will be discussed in more detail later. Because to the majority of people, flowers are the most important, we will consider those that bloom in the shade. What are the perennials, annuals, and shrubs that actually flower when deprived, in varying degrees, of the life-giving sun? But first, what are the varying degrees?

Shade is usually caused by trees and buildings. Except in a poorly situated city garden, the shade cast by buildings or solid masses of trees, where there is direct sunlight only three to six hours a day, is partial shade. The shade of a building is usually on the north side. Whatever is planted there receives a few hours of morning sunlight and shade the rest of the day — or a few hours of sunlight in the afternoon.

Usually there are light and air around a building, and they are almost as good for some plants as direct sunlight. If there is a building overlooking our garden, we must choose plants that grow with plenty of light and air, yet only a few hours of direct sunlight.

The shade cast by trees and shrubbery can be a very dense shade. It can be smothering if the branches are low and the leaves thick. This is worse for plants than shade cast by buildings because of lack of air circulation. Very few plants can survive it, although I have had *Pachysandra* and *Phlox stolonifera* thrive under honeysuckle bushes that were under branches of Red Maple trees.

Even in nature plants do not grow well in dense shade. The best evergreen lumber trees are those that have grown up as a compact forest, crowding out other growth, and killing off side branches so knots will not develop. For certain purposes, that is good; but it is bad for the individual tree and for the few ferns and wild flowers that have the strength to push down roots under them. The shade on that forest floor is so dense that even at high noon, the light is bleakly gray.

More plants would start growing, however, were it not for the thick carpet of needles and branches. The impetus to survive is stubborn and unyielding. Roots reach an unbelievable distance to find nourishment; stems grow lanky and anemic in seeking the sun. There is occasionally an extreme case of a plant's living without sunlight, like the little fern I once saw growing deep in a Missouri cavern. Its only light was a single electric light bulb.

To be happy, both plants and humans must have sun (in varying degrees) as well as water, air, and food. Crowding is not good for individuals, even if those individuals are trees. Of whatever use they might be to man, they do not develop to their fullest beauty when growing too close to their neighbors. The weakest trees inevitably suffer and usually die out.

If the trees in your yard grow within a few feet of each other, you will have to choose between an emaciated woodland with little undergrowth or weeding out a few trees. Better to eliminate spindling saplings and give room to promising ones. From the larger trees, select those that are most apt to develop into beautiful specimens situated where you want them, and cut down the others. That is good for the trees and lets in sunlight and air to the gardens you want to develop beneath them.

From large established trees, whose roots will allow a garden, you might want to cut off a few lower branches. Give your plants in the shade as much light and air as possible without sacrificing the beauty above them. However, low branches of trees such as Maples and Beeches, whose roots rob the soil of food and water, and consequently allow few other plants to linger in the competition for survival, might well be left on to hide the bare earth beneath.

For our purposes a dense shade is cast by the massed shadows of large trees, the shadows of buildings and trees, or by high, impenetrable hedges. It is not a desirable shade in which to grow plants or establish a garden, but the situation occurs now and then and we must make the best of it. When you are told that flowers will bloom in the shade, choose

plants which naturally enjoy shade. Don't start out with
Petunias or Portulaca, and be disappointed at their scraggly
growth. They are essentially sun-lovers, and must have the
sun so that their leaves can manufacture the right amount
of food to enable them to fulfill their life mission — of reproducing their kind. Self-sown seedlings of Petunias and other
sun-lovers occasionally survive in a little light shade, if you
keep the plants pinched back, but as a rule they prefer the
sun.

Light shade is actually what most people mean when they
talk about gardening in the shade, although it is difficult to
separate the varying degrees of sunlight and shadow. Dense
shade in the morning might be light shade by afternoon or
even bright sunlight. I think of light shade as the shade under
high-arched branches of surrounding trees where direct sunlight occasionally hits.

Spattered sunlight is also the shade under tall trees, but
it is a more enduring shade than light shade. Direct sunlight
seldom reaches it for long at a time; when it does, it usually
sifts down between leafy branches. At noon it may be bright
with sunbeams, and breezes will gently stir the growths beneath, but there will be no hot sun. Many so-called "sun-
loving" plants, such as perennial garden Phlox, Tansy, etc.,
will tolerate light shade and spattered sunlight.

In my garden there are mostly White Pines, Oaks, and
Locusts, so I have all degrees of shade. Even my sunny garden
is in shadow much of the time, particularly in late summer
and fall as the sun travels more toward the south. But plants
thrive there because there is plenty of humus in the soil and
plenty of light and air. About half my garden is in light shade,
and the area around the Shady Rock Garden receives spattered sunlight — only a few hours of direct sunlight at certain

times of the year. Here is where ferns flourish, and the little spring wild flowers, along with ground covers, a few evergreens, and many varieties of *Hosta*.

Sometimes the problem is not one of shade at all. It is a problem of roots. Under trees whose tap roots travel deep into the earth and whose lateral roots keep pretty much to themselves, there is only the work of planting between the roots. Those of Oaks, Pines, and other evergreens are easily detected and circumvented. Locusts, Sassafras, established Dogwoods and Birches have numerous small roots that can be planted around or occasionally cut away, if you add plenty of humus as food for the remaining neighboring roots.

It is the large, sprawling trees that cause the most trouble — Maples, Beeches, Elms; and Lindens, to a lesser degree. Their roots stretch out like a fine network across the top of the soil, usually to the width of their branch-spread. Fertilizer and moisture added to the soil only encourage more roots. Grass seldom thrives under those trees; perennials do not like them at all; only shallow-rooted ground-covers have the courage to defy them. But I have maintained a garden in the shade made by a house and six large elm trees, but away from the roots. I have seen a whole shrub-bank under a Beech tree, and as green a lawn as you would ever wish to see, carpeting the ground beneath three large Red Maples. Inquiring of the gardeners who were responsible for the latter two phenomena, I learned that the shrubs were replanted every few years, the tree-roots being cut away and replaced with good soil and fertilizer. The Maple trees had three feet of loam over their roots, due to a filling project.

Nothing is more beautiful than a mature Beech tree, a spreading Sugar Maple with its brilliant fall coloring, or a gnarled Live Oak, but what is to be done when grass refuses to grow over their roots? On some trees you can leave on the lower branches, like petticoats, to hide the nude earth beneath. Under others you can make a terrace where you can relax and look at bits of sky between the twisting branches. Most trees can stand a flagstone, or even a paved terrace. Leave an area around the trunk for expansion and water seepage. Set furniture on the terrace, and arrange your flower gardens at the outside edges of the terrace away from the tree-roots.

When there is root interference from small trees and rooty shrubs, use a root-restrainer. This usually consists of a strip of metal about two feet high, sunk into the earth in front of the wandering roots. In front of this wall, flowering plants no longer have extra roots with which to contend and can flourish. This method is used a great deal in the South where a little shade is almost a necessity in order to have a garden at all; it is used in the North to restrain soil-robbers like Privet and Lilacs.

It is difficult to know, merely from suggestions and accounts of other people's experiences, just what you can grow in your shady garden. The best thing to do is to keep trying different shade-tolerant plants in different locations until you find the ideal spot. Someone has said that gardening consists of moving "this," here, so "that" can go over there. It is even truer when one gardens in the shade.

Most fun in gardening comes in moving things about. Anyone can weed, but to determine when a plant is not happy and to give it more, or less, shade; to find that one plant is too tall and to move it to the background while supplying it with the correct amount of sun and other requirements; to fill an empty space with the right plant that blossoms at the right time; to arrange flower colors and contrasting foliage so they make the most pleasing pictures; that is gardening!

Move things about for experimental purposes. Sometimes the results will be surprising; sometimes disappointing; but always interesting.

1. Many sun-loving plants will tolerate light shade or spattered sunlight.

2. In shade, blossoms are usually larger and deeper in color.

3. Plant-development in the shade is often behind that of the same varieties growing in full sunlight.

4. Stems of sun-loving plants, growing in the shade, are usually weak.

5. Self-sown seedlings of certain plants will tolerate more shade than transplanted seedlings.

6. Yellow, white, and pink flowers bring out the shadows and give greater depth to the shady garden.

7. To thrive in the shade, sun-preferring plants must have an over-abundance of other requirements — more air, more moisture, more food. In nature, most plants that bloom in the shade have an abundance of one, or more, of these essentials.

8. Compost and leafmold are necessary to the shady garden, not only adding nutrients, but building up the soil to better retain moisture.

2

Spring Wild Flowers That Like Shade

✤✻✥✿✱✻✥✿✱✻✥✿✱✻✥✿✱✻✥✿✱✻✥✿✱✻✥✿✱✻✥✿✱✻✥✿✱✻✥✿

WHEN PEOPLE SPEAK of a wild-flower garden they usually mean a wooded section of their yard given over to the growing of those appealing little flowers found blooming in the woods in spring. Actually all plants were once "wild."

The originals of plants that we assemble in our gardens in America might have come from any place in the world. We have adopted a number from the Orient, such as Forsythia and Peonies; others come from South Africa (*Saintpaulia*); others from Mexico, and still others are from different parts of our own country. Because they are new to us, and different from our local native plants, we think of them as something special.

Local native wild flowers should be treated as something special, too. It takes a special kind of gardener to recognize, and lead others to recognize, their natural simple beauty. Perhaps their rise in popularity is a matter of scarcity, leading to demand. It may be a belated appreciation born of the fear of losing something. At any rate, many gardeners now plan a corner of their yards as a wild-flower garden.

Along with this interest in native wild plants comes a curiosity about growing wild flowers from other places. These are usually referred to as "species," which is the original plant as grown by nature (in comparison to hybrids or varieties). A group of species with similar characteristics comprises a Genus. A number of Genera make up a Family. An example is the dainty little Candy-stick Tulip *(Tulipa Clusiana)* — a wild plant from Portugal — of the *Genus* Tulipa, *Species* Clusiana. Its common name, Candy-stick Tulip, comes from its red and white stripes. *Eichleri,* with pert, pointed petals of bright red, is a wild flower from Asia. There are species *Narcissi* too, such as *Narcissus Bulbocodium* from North Africa; and species, or wild, Iris *(Iris reticulata)*.

All these species could be included in the wild-flower garden, but for the sake of those with a fixed idea of a wild-flower garden, we will list here only those early-blooming, woodsy wild flowers native to our country or locale.

Perhaps you will recognize some as flowers you discovered on childhood rambles in the woods, although woods, as most of us have known them in the past, are growing scarce. Many woodlands are retained by private individuals who often post NO TRESPASSING signs, and with good reasons.

People are apt to think that wild flowers are theirs simply for the taking. So they dig them up or pull them by the roots to get the flowers, often destroying in a moment what has taken nature years to accomplish. This has happened to the native hollies in New England *(Ilex opaca* and *I. verticillata),* and to Trailing Arbutus, which has disappeared from some regions entirely. Garden clubs have had these plants placed on Conservation lists in an effort to make people aware of their beauty and the need to save them, and they encourage people to include wild-flower garden areas in their own gardens and to buy seeds and plants from nurseries rather than dig them from the wild.

More than most other plants, the spring wild flowers must have large quantities of leafmold and humus in the soil in order to thrive. They like moisture and the shade of tall trees. Most of them require an acid soil (see Chapter 17) or some other soil conditions of which the amateur usually is not aware. If you are lucky enough to find Dutchman's Breeches, Hepatica, or some other wild flower growing in its native habitat, and you are allowed to dig it up, take particular notice of its surroundings. What kinds of trees branch over it? How dense is the shade? In what kind of soil is it growing? Wet or dry — light or heavy? If you can duplicate the conditions in your own yard, good. If not, leave the wild flowers alone, to continue to flourish and bloom for other eager flower-hunters.

Some wild flowers will survive almost any kind of conditions. Violets, barring a few exceptions (notably, the Birdsfoot Violet, which needs an acid soil in a sunny location), will grow anywhere. Most of them love moisture, but survive in dry places. They endure sun and shade and bloom in either. They do not seem to care whether the soil is rich or poor. For the beginner, violets make an excellent start.

Other wild flowers are not so adaptable. Some must have swampy conditions (Marsh-Marigold). Others must have dry hillsides. Some are choosy about their trees, such as Pink Lady-Slipper with its preference for Hemlocks and White

Pines. Others like the companionship of Oaks or a mixture of Oaks and evergreens. Few flowers grow under Maples because Maple roots are soil-robbers and will not tolerate plants near them with any root-depth. Few wild flowers bloom in shade that is very dense. They prefer open woods, usually of mixed trees where stray rays of sunlight filter across them during the day. Remember this, and either thin out a thick grove of trees or use only a few trees under which to establish your wild garden.

Save the fallen leaves from those trees to return to the soil in the form of leafmold. In their natural state, woodsy wild flowers thrive on decomposing forest litter that has been allowed to remain as it fell. This decomposing litter makes a humus-mulch which feeds the plants and builds up the soil so it retains necessary moisture. Duplicating as nearly as possible the native home of wild flowers is a long step toward ultimate success in establishing a wild-flower garden. For further success, begin with flowers that are easy to grow.

Attractive little Dutchman's Breeches with lacy foliage and creamy white flowers actually resembling a line of pantaloons hung to dry, grows in either a heavy or light soil. With plenty of humus, and sometimes in an almost dense shade, it thrives and increases happily with the years. *Iris cristata* seems to be at home anywhere, sun or shade. *Mertensia* comes up year after year with little care and attention. Solomon's Seal is a vigorous plant and stands mediocre soil and conditions; but given a woodsy home with humus, it flourishes, often attaining a height of three feet.

Success with these will lead you to try some of the more difficult plants like Bunchberry and *Shortia galacifolia,* which must have an acid soil. You will want to try Lady-Slippers too. The little yellow one *(Cypripedium pubescens)* is a delightful

charmer and easiest to establish of all the native orchids. The
pink one (*C. acaule*) is more choosy, but both need plenty
of humus. If you have a rocky ledge in partial shade, you will
want American Columbine (*Aquilegia canadensis*), which
likes a poor rocky soil, on the dry side.

Most wild flowers grow from a bulbous or rhizomatous
rootstock and are best planted in the fall. Directions for planting usually accompany orders from a nursery, for each wild
flower has its preference as to the depth the root should go.
Usually such things as *Mertensia* and Jack-in-the-Pulpit are
placed an inch or so below the top of the ground. *Iris cristata*
likes its rhizomes almost at the top of the soil, with roots going
deeper, although it is such an agreeable plant that it survives
almost any kind of planting and adjusts its roots accordingly.
Pink Lady-Slipper roots reach a depth of 6 to 8 inches. The
roots of Solomon's Seal too, reach a good depth, in order to
to serve as anchor for the sturdy stalks. Some of the wild Lily
bulbs growing at the edges of our woodlands are even deeper,
and many a Lily is lost because people break the stalk from
the bulb in an effort to dig it up.

If you purchase wild flowers from a nearby nursery
(always better practice if you can manage it), you can often
acquire them in spring with a good-sized clump of earth.
Such things as the white Canada Violet, *Phlox divaricata,* and
Foam Flower have creeping roots near the surface and are
easily moved almost any time. Arbutus is easily moved with a
generous clump of soil, but it must have its native woodsy
conditions duplicated.

Before planting wild flowers, very poor soil should be
dug out and replaced with a good deal of leafmold mixed
with a little of the soil. If it is heavy and rather clayey, mix
in a little sand to promote drainage. In spite of the fact that

Phlox divaricata can be used to brighten up tree roots.

many wild flowers seem to grow in swamp-land, there are few under cultivation that will stand having wet feet all the time.

Dig your hole large enough to take in the whole clump of roots without crowding. Don't be afraid of having the surrounding soil mixed with rough compost. Wild flowers love it. They also like a light mulch of partly decomposed compost or leafmold, or pine needles all the time. This helps duplicate the natural soil conditions under which they live. Some of the evergreen varieties, like Arbutus, must have their foliage protected against late winter winds. In some areas where it grows naturally, this is taken care of by snow, but where the snowfall is light, and where the foliage is exposed to the weather, it should be covered with pine boughs (letting in the air but keeping out the wind), or other suitable covering that will not mat down and smother the plant.

Wild flowers are tall, intermediate, low-growing, or ground-cover types. Study their habits of growth and types of foliage to determine where they will best fit into your design.

Tall Solomon's Seal is naturally a background plant used with other wild flowers. It will hold its own against taller shrubbery, but is graceful and lovely used alone in front of a wall. Bellwort (*Uvularia*), more slender and delicate of stem, but with a similar manner of growing, can be used by itself in a clump, or in colonies among a ground cover of wild Lily-of-the-Valley or Checkerberry. *Mertensia* foliage and that of Dutchman's Breeches die down after blooming and should be placed behind ferns or other plants which will hide the dying foliage. Most of the Lady-Slippers have good foliage and seem at their best in groups of their own kind. *Trillium grandi-*

florum makes a spectacular showing in large colonies, but the smaller Trilliums are more attractive in modest clumps beside rocks or fallen logs. Most of the violets are good foliage plants, have attractive blossoms as well, and are useful in all sorts of places.

In planting a wild garden, try to build up groups with contrasting forms and different foliage. The heavy bold leaves of the Pink Lady-Slipper make a good foil for the hairy heart-shaped foliage of Foam Flower. The umbrella-like leaves of the May Apple are so large as to appear almost tropical among other wild flowers; it is better in colonies by itself or growing under, or near shrubs and small trees. Pipsissewa, with leathery leaves in irregular whorls, is lovely as a ground cover under pines, or can be used as an accent plant among other creeping plants like Partridge-Berry. Almost any of the wild flowers can be used in groups to enhance a natural rock ledge or boulder beside a path, to dress up an old stump, or simply to be themselves among the dry, brown leaves.

Wherever they are planted, there is a rewarding delight in growing wild flowers. A very shady area can be completely turned over to them. Though you have cleared out special sunny spots for rose beds and annuals, keep a small shaded plot for wild flowers.

SPRING WILD FLOWERS THAT LIKE SHADE

Achlys triphylla — Deer-Foot. Western wild flower found in shady woods. Fan-shaped leaflets, spiky blossoms. Interesting. Delicate.

Actaea alba; rubra — White and Red Baneberry. To 18″. Terminal clusters of small white flowers developing into effective white or red berries in late summer. Light to heavy shade.

Anemone quinquefolia — Dainty Wood Anemone to 8". Solitary white flower growing from apex of 3-5 parted leaves. Sometimes called "Wind Flower" because it is supposed to open at the wind's bidding.

Aquilegia canadensis — Wild Columbine. Dainty, but wiry; red and yellow blossoms growing in rocky soil in sun or shade. *A. caerulea* is Western species (Colorado state flower). Showy blue or white flowers.

Arisaema triphyllum — Jack-in-the-Pulpit. Dearly-loved oddity of the wild garden. Likes humus. In shade, the foliage remains in good condition.

Asarum canadense — Wild Ginger. Odd, dark-brown curled flowers amid kidney-shaped leaves. Interesting as low spot near a pool. Rich humus.

Caltha palustris — Marsh-Marigold. Shining, yellow, buttercup-like flowers. Likes wet woodlands, but will adapt to moist soil with plenty of humus.

Campanula rotundifolia — Bluebells of Scotland. Slender, wiry stems with dainty blue bell-like flowers in June and throughout summer. Rocky woods. Open shade.

Caulophyllum thalictroides — Blue Cohosh. Dainty foliage in spring. Blue berries. Partial shade in rich soil.

Chamaelirium luteum — Fairywand. Tuberous-rooted plant to 4'. For the back of the wild garden or at edge of stream or pond. Spike-like sprays of blossoms of yellowish white. Moist, peaty soil in light shade.

Chimaphila umbellata — Pipsissewa. Small evergreen herbs with attractive, glossy foliage. Nodding umbels of pink or white flowers in summer, but included here because they seem to belong to the wild garden. *C. maculata* has variegated foliage and fragrant flowers.

Claytonia virginica — Spring Beauty. Low-growing plant with grass-like leaves. Pink and white blossoms. Likes moist humus in partial shade.

Clintonia borealis — Shiny, broad basal leaves. Yellowish bell-like flowers followed by handsome blue berries. This and Western species with rose-purple flowers must have cool, moist woods in order to bloom.

Coptis trifolia — Goldthread, from the yellow, bitter roots. Low-growing. White or yellow flowers. Likes damp woods, but must have coolness in order to bloom.

Cornus canadensis — Bunchberry. To 8″. White, typical dogwood flower with 4 bracts surrounding a dense head of pale flowers. Handsome red berries. Half shade, acid soil, lots of humus.

Bunchberry (*Cornus canadensis*) is difficult
to grow, but is worth the effort.

Hepatica is one of the first spring flowers.

Cypripedium parviflorum — Yellow Lady-Slipper. Charming. Easiest of all Lady-Slippers to grow. Any soil. *C. acaule* — Pink Lady-Slipper. Acid soil with plenty of humus. Probably needs association with white pines or hemlocks.

Dentaria diphylla — Toothwort, because of tooth-like roots that are good in salads. To 10″. Flowers, usually white, in terminal clusters. Light, rich soil. One-half to light shade. *D. laciniata.* Que. to Minn., and Fla.

Dicentra canadensis — Squirrel-Corn, from roots in small tubers. Loose spray of greenish white flowers. Dainty, attractive. Light rich soil; *right* degree of shade.

Dicentra Cucullaria — Dutchman's-Breeches. To 10″. Delicate foliage. Creamy white blossoms, like miniature pantaloons hung on a line. Foliage dies in summer.

Dodecatheon Meadia — Shooting-Star. Pink or pinkish flowers resemble a bunch of "shooting stars" at end of stem to 18″ long. Intriguing. Moderately rich soil, well-drained. Will bloom with very little sun, but must have air circulation.

Epigaea repens — Trailing Arbutus. Trailing evergreen of the Heath Family. Acid soil; plenty of humus. Protection from winds. Clusters of pinkish flowers have exquisite fragrance.

Epipactis pubescens — Rattlesnake-Plaintain. Hardy terrestrial orchid. Leaves veined white. Orchid-like blossoms in terminal spike. Acid, leafmold.

Erythronium americanum — Dog-Tooth Violet. Speckled leaves. Small, lily-like flower of soft yellow. Likes plenty of compost in light shade. Western species grow in cool woods. *E. albidum*. White, pink or purplish.

Galax aphylla — Galax. Shiny, rounded leaves, bronzy during fall and winter. Fine for corsages. Graceful spike of white flowers to 14″. Sandy loam with humus. Protect from rabbits.

Gaultheria procumbens — Wintergreen. Oval, leathery leaves. Nodding white flowers followed by scarlet fruits. Acid soil.

Hepatica triloba — Liverleaf. Light to deep shade. Three-lobed leaves green through winter. Blue, pink, or white blossoms, very early. Attractive. Neutral soil with plenty of humus. Does not like to be disturbed. *H. acutiloba,* pointed leaf-lobes.

Houstonia caerulea — Bluets. Low, tufted. Will take light shade, but prefers the open. Charming. Var. Millards, tiny, with profusion of blue stars.

Hypoxis hirsuta — Yellow Star-Grass. Interesting. Pretty. Likes dry shade; poor, rocky soil. Do not mistake for grass, when not in flower.

(*Paul E. Genereux*)

Galax likes shade in summer and an acid soil.

Iris cristata — Native of Southern Mountains, but hardy. To 8″. Delightful. Early bloomer. Deep shade. *I. verna,* smaller.

Jeffersonia diphylla — Twin-Leaf. Grows to 1′. Two-parted leaves; dainty white flowers, 1″ across. Easily grown in rich humus.

Linnaea borealis — Twin-Flower. Dainty, trailing evergreen; pink, bell-shaped, fragrant flowers. New England and North. Acid soil, rich in leafmold.

Maianthemum canadense — False Lily-of-the-Valley. Leaves like miniature lily-of-the-valley leaves. Small white flowers in a terminal raceme. Makes excellent ground cover for the wild garden in cool parts of the country.

Mitchella repens — Partridge-Berry . Attractive evergreen vine. Pinkish white blossoms have delightful fragrance. Half and light shade. Humus. Spectacular red berries.

Mitella diphylla — Common Mitrewort. Heart-shaped, basal leaves. Spikes of small greenish flowers. Rich leafmold in half and light shade.

Myosotis laxa — Forget-Me-Not. Any varieties fit into the wild garden or any other garden. This is found on muddy banks and swamps but will grow in loose, humusy soil and blooms from June on.

Oakesia sessilifolia (*Uvularia sessilifolia*) — Common Bellwort. Dainty. Graceful, creamy yellow bells. Grows anywhere.

Oxalis acetosella — Wood-Sorrel. Dainty pink and white flowers in clover-like leaves. Cool woods. Humusy, acid soil.

Phlox divaricata — See Chapter 3.

Podophyllum peltatum — May-Apple. Large, umbrella-like leaves with creamy white flowers in the fork of the leaf-stem. Grows anywhere in partial shade. Takes over in good soil. Interesting.

Polygala paucifolia — Flowering Wintergreen. Flowers, like tiny rose orchids in axils of upper leaves. Low-growing. Partial and light shade. Acid soil.

Polygonatum biflorum — Solomon's-Seal. Graceful, curving stem to 3'. Bell-like flowers along it on the under sides. Interesting. Spectacular, in the wild garden or other places. Thrives in humus.

Pyrola rotundifolia — Shinleaf. Likes poor, sandy soil, but it must be acid. Shining, rounded evergreen leaves with pretty white stalk of flowers in summer.

Sanguinaria canadensis — Bloodroot (from red juice of root and stem). Wild garden favorite with snow-white blossoms and deeply lobed leaves. Usual rich woodland soil.

Saxifraga virginiensis — Saxifrage; Rosette of leaves. Small white flowers clustered at top of stem. Likes rocky soil.

Shortia galacifolia — Oconee-Bells. Delightful, early-blooming, white bell-like flowers. Grows beautifully when once established. Compost and acid soil.

Smilacina racemosa — False Solomon's-Seal. Similar to Solomon's Seal, except flowers in terminal spike. Fruits, red. Good for flower arrangements. Light shade, any good soil.

Stylophorum diphyllum — Celandine-Poppy. To 1'. Handsome, pinnately-parted foliage. Yellow flowers to 2" across. Clumps in wild garden or shady perennial garden.

Tellima grandiflora — False Alum-Root. Western counterpart of Mitella. Greenish flowers with fringed petals. Charming in the wild garden. Moist soil, rich in humus, partial shade.

Tiarella cordifolia — Foam-Flower. Fluffy raceme of white flowers. Leaves somewhat heart-shaped. Spreads quickly to good ground-cover in summer. Easily grown in colonies.

Trientalis borealis — Starflower. To 8". Small white flower like a star on a whorl of green pointed leaves. Slender, delicate stem. Likes rich, shady woods.

Trillium grandiflorum — Spectacular long-lasting white blossoms, well above three-parted leaves. Shady, moist soil rich in humus, grows easily, even in city gardens. *T. erectum,* purplish red; *T. undulatum,* Painted Trillium.

Uvularia grandiflora — Great Merry-Bells. Bellwort. Larger than *Oakesia,* with bells of clearer yellow. Easily grown in humusy soil.

Viola — Wild species too numerous for listing. *V. canadensis*, creamy white Canadian violet; *V. blanda,* white swamp violet; *V. pubescens,* downy, yellow violet for dry, rich woods; *V. papilionacea,* common blue violet, and many others, most of them easy to grow in any soil, and a delight, although some are weedy.

3

Other Spring Perennials That Like Shade

~✦❋✦❀✦❋✦❀✦❋✦❀✦❋✦❀✦❋✦❀✦❋✦❀✦❋✦❀✦❋✦❀✦❋✦❀✦❋✦❀✦❋✦❀✦❋✦❀✦❋✦❀✦

IT IS DIFFICULT to separate some of the wild flowers from those we call "cultivated," or "garden" flowers. Many species, especially those that bloom in the spring, are much the same as they were when discovered by Linnaeus, Michaux, Fortune, Gray, or other wild-flower explorers. Yet, because we have never found them in the wild, or because we grow them in our gardens, we think of them as "cultivated," and give them a place in the perennial border, or rock garden, instead of in the corner devoted to the small, spring-blooming wild flowers like *Hepatica* and Bloodroot.

Jacob's Ladder *(Polemonium)* for instance, is used as a cultivated spring flower, good for rock gardens and partly-shaded areas that are not too dry. Yet the *Polemonium* in my garden seems exactly the same as the wild species I found blooming in mid-July, high in a Wyoming canyon. The season of bloom was different, of course, inasmuch as blooming

30

time varies with climate, altitude, location, and even exposures in the same garden.

Columbine (*Aquilegia*) is both a wild and a cultivated flower; the wild usually is considered the delicate little red species, *Aquilegia canadensis*. But there are wild white and blue Columbines too. Several are indigenous to the areas stretching from Montana to New Mexico, and have quite a cultivated look because of their robust habits and attractive starry flowers. It is thought that these species, as well as European and Oriental Columbines, are represented in some of the exquisite hybrids that we enjoy as "cultivated" Aquilegias.

Most of the spring-blooming flowers that tolerate shade are low-growing. Consequently, they are used in shady rock-gardens, on the top of walls, around pools, and in front of the perennial border. Those with foliage remaining attractive all summer (*Epimedium, Pulmonaria,* etc.) can be planted among evergreen shrubs, or in the foundation planting. Some of them, with neat, pretty foliage like Coral Bells (*Heuchera*) make good edging plants for a shady corner. Others are better accents. Still others, like *Iris cristata,* serve several purposes; embellishing the wild garden, beautifying the perennial border, or acting as a ground cover for shrubs.

These plants, along with most early spring wild flowers, are perennials; that is, they die back to the roots each fall and send up new growth in the spring. Well-planted, in good soil, and given average care, they come up year after year.

For a shady garden, especially where space is limited, choose perennials that offer interesting form and foliage as well as good blossoming habits. Let them add to the garden-picture throughout the whole season. There will be some

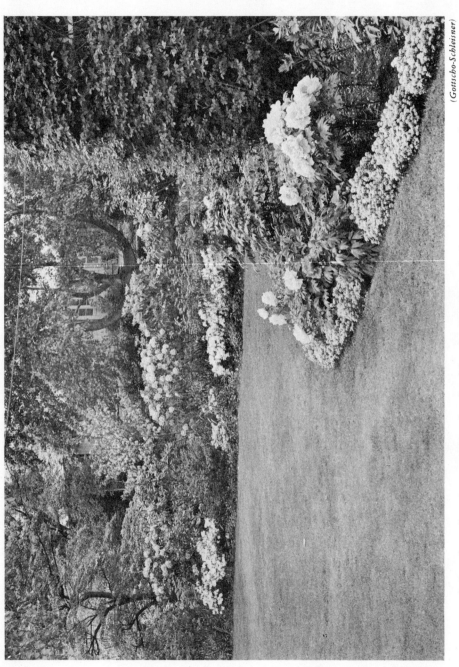

A border of tree peonies, edged with candytuft, and rhododendrons and azalea in the rear, makes a riot of color in the spring.

desirable flowers that cannot do this — bulbs, for instance — yet we could not garden without our spring bells and trumpets. Bulb-foliage, and that of *Mertensia, Ranunculus ficaria* and others, dies down after the plants have blossomed; but ferns and other shrubby foliage planted in front of them will keep the garden trim and neat.

Perennials are frequently planted in a long, rectangular flower bed known as a perennial border. This may stand in the middle of a lawn by itself, or at the edge of a lawn, against a fence, wall, shrubs, trees, or some other background where the flowers can show to the best advantage. Where there is a background of trees or shrubs, separate the perennials from the trees by a path — or at least a space — so that the plants can have as much sun- and root-room as possible.

Against a wall or fence, plants over 12" high should be far enough in front so that they seem in the right proportion — a foot or so from a low wall or fence, a little further away if the wall is higher. This depends, of course, on the type of wall or fence, the width of the flower bed, and the other plants it contains, as well as the distance from which they are to be viewed. But the relationship of background and plants is important. In the shade, the green of trees and shrubs makes an ideal background for tall, light-colored flowers. Garden Phlox, for instance, can be lost in a battle of magentas, and pinks, and salmons. Separate some of the lush colors by green or white or set them against a background of green.

Early spring-blooming perennials, most of which are low-growing, have the advantage of long stretches of bare earth to serve as their backgrounds. Or they bloom against a shrub, or the green of a higher-growing perennial. Many times a spring flower is at its best befriending a rock ledge or enhancing a piece of driftwood. A low stone-wall is an ideal background for some of the small spring blossoms, either planted against it or on top, tumbling down over the stones. If you have no rock wall, you might want a few perennials around a tree, its trunk serving as the background. Trees make focal points too, for garden areas built with shrubs, perennials, and a few well-chosen annuals that don't mind shade.

Spring blossoms are not usually flamboyant. The colors are soft and tend to blend. Nevertheless, a gardener with an eye to form and color, is always rearranging his plants to make more beautiful garden pictures. Pink Tulips courting Wild Blue Phlox! A brown-leaved woodland punctuated with Narcissi and Daffodils! Purple Aubrietia draping the shoulders of a gray rock! Try to arrange your spring flowers in the most effective combinations. Set them off, together or separately, with the neutral tones of rocks, dried leaves, old wood, or the green of grass and trees.

In planting perennials follow the same general rules for design that you would follow in planting shrubs. Tall plants are placed toward the back, or in the center of a free-standing bed, as skyline accents at strategic points. Intermediate, or shrubby types, are used as "fillers"; with low-growing plants in front, either as edging plants or focal points.

It is not always possible to place shrubs or perennials in a definite category, however, because what one plant does in one location, might not be possible in another. A 9′ Arborvitae might be built down by a clump of Black Snakeroot (*Cimicifuga racemosa*) acting as a "filler" between the Arborvitae and a low, shrubby Astilbe. In a totally different picture, the *Cimicifuga* instead of the Arborvitae might serve as the background plant. Siberian Iris might then act as the "filler," with a focal point of *Bergenia*.

In a shady corner, the red-brown branches of Sweet Pepperbush give height and background to Yellow Lady-Slippers planted among the unfolding fronds of Maidenhair Fern. Later, when the Sweet Pepperbush is in leaf, the fern foliage

(*Paul E. Genereux*)

A spring garden with a brook and a stone wall, featuring March Marigolds, Primula, Forget-Me-Nots, Daffodils and other plants in a naturalistic setting.

is a lacy platform holding it to the earth. To the right of this
picture, the planting might be continued with a ground cover
of airy *Epimedium,* punctuated with *Ilex crenata,* whose
glossy evergreen outfit makes a good accent for winter. Camellias, on the other hand, with larger, shiny leaves near the
ground, would ask nothing more than a ground-cover, the
Camellia branches themselves serving as "filler" material.

Time of bloom makes a difference in the purpose for
which a perennial is chosen. A garden might be so arranged
that the white summer-blooming *Lysimachia clethroides*
would bloom against a Fir, Hemlock, or other triangular evergreen. Yet, all during the growing season the *Lysimachia*
foliage would be attractive opposition to the evergreen needles. Coral Bells placed at the front of the planting can give
spring blossom-interest as well as additional foliage contrast
during the summer. Whorled Aster and Blue Lobelia can
also serve as "filler" plants during their growing periods. They
are shrubby and green in a clump, their freshness of bloom in
late summer is welcome when so much of the garden is de-
pleted.

In a free-standing flower bed, with no definite background, the tallest plants are usually placed in the middle
of the bed, and "stepped down" by means of intermediate, or
filler plants. This usually means a more formal pattern, edged
with a low border of plants. Unity in such a bed, or in any
sizable garden is achieved by means of a "theme" — clumps
of tall-growing perennials spaced at more or less regular intervals to give continuity. In a border garden, tall plants are
accents toward the back, either against a fence, wall, or other
definite background, or as a background themselves. Here,
too, use them in clumps at regular intervals, so that the eye
will be carried along from plant to plant.

In conjunction with these background plants, intermediate or filler plants are staggered between and in front of the tall plants. Never set one plant directly in front of another. These filler plants are similar in size and form; and sometimes, in a narrow flower bed, can serve as the background plants.

This simplified planting is the skeleton of any garden design. Dress it up with other plants chosen carefully for color, foliage, and ability to withstand your conditions of shade. Tuck in something unusual here and there. Play up a mound of bright spring color. Add spiky Iris foliage for contrast. Let the bold round leaves of *Petasites* startle you. Plant Sweet Violets and *Hesperis* for fragrance. But remember, as you plant, that these are merely frills embellishing your basic pattern. Garden harmony is achieved by a certain amount of repetition. Too many different plants result in a hodge-podge.

Usually with shade limitations there is not much opportunity for free-standing flower beds large enough to hold many background clumps. In a garden under trees, or near buildings, a perennial border would probably be partly in the sun. In this case the gardener naturally places the sun-loving plants where they will grow best, and devotes the rest of the border to those that will stand the degree of shade in the particular spot, following rules of design as far as he is able. No one can tell how much sun or shade a garden receives except the one who works in it; he must keep experimenting with various shade-tolerant plants of adequate height, color, and soil-demands until he finds the right ones for his particular garden.

Although the best time to separate spring-blooming perennials is directly after they have bloomed or in the fall, almost any plant can be moved in the spring provided enough care is taken. Spring is the active growing season and nature cooperates in getting plants established.

To plant, dig a space large enough to take care of the

(Gottscho-Schleisner)

Bleeding heart, foam flower and *Phlox divaricata*.

whole clump without crowding. At the bottom of the hole (particularly if your soil is as poor as it is in most places) dig in 1–4 quarts of compost from your compost pile. Add a little rotted manure (if available) and 2–4 tablespoons of bone meal, if your plant is not an acid-lover, and several inches of topsoil. Water, if dry. Set in the clump so that the neck of the plant comes even with the ground level. Work in more compost and soil around the outside edges of the clump, pushing the soil in around plant so that the clump sets firmly. Water well, if needed. Keep covered until the plant is established. Water during dry spells. If you choose a rainy spell for your planting, you can probably forget covering and the first watering.

Moving a clump of spring-blooming perennials whose roots have spread unchecked is a little different. Fall is a better time for doing this although it may be done successfully in early spring. Some plants are agreeable to being moved any time; others recover quickly, although naturally all plants resent having their roots torn from the soil and need time to reestablish themselves. If a plant is temperamental, the flowers and buds should be removed after transplanting so that the strength can go to root development instead of to the plant's natural function of reproducing itself through blossoms and seeds. A good root system ensures a healthy plant.

As you become more discriminating in your choice of plant material, you will find yourself "swapping" with other discriminating gardeners, or having to order from a specialized nursery the more unusual plants. Plant-quarantines and other restrictions prohibit large clumps of earth around roots, and the plant will arrive from the nursery with bare roots wrapped in clean, damp moss and exuding an aroma of disinfectant. If the roots are at all dry, soak them for several hours or overnight. If not, get the plant into the ground as soon as possible. Plant according to directions above, working in good topsoil well around the roots. Do not add fertilizer. Give the plant a chance to get established before feeding it. If it looks a little sad, set a strawberry box covered with a polyethylene bag over it (no holes in the bag). Or plant it in full shade and cover with a large glass jar, keeping the soil damp but not wet. If it dies and you think it the fault of the nursery, notify them immediately. Reliable plant houses usually take care of such losses.

All this discussion has been in relation to moving spring-blooming perennials in the spring. Separating plants, as well as major transplanting jobs which involve breaking up a clump, should be done after a plant has bloomed, usually in late summer. This is a good general rule, although the exact time of dividing depends on the plant, the weather, and your own convenience. Siberian Iris, for example, which blooms after the Bearded Irises, can be separated immediately after blooming, but some people prefer separating it in late summer with cooler days.

Such shade-loving plants as *Pulmonaria, Epimedium,* and Canadian Violets, which bloom April–May, need to be separated and replanted only when their clumps grow too large for the territory, when they do not bloom well, or show other signs of maladjustment. In dividing them, give individual plants plenty of room in which to spread and grow. Dig humus into the soil. These plants need humus and the aeration it provides. If their roots are crowded in a dense soil they do not receive proper air circulation or enough moisture to allow the root hairs to absorb nourishment. Compost does not have to be fully decomposed to provide humus for your plants. Many prefer it "in the rough," with leaves, etc., only partly broken up. It is then that the soil bacteria and other micro-organisms do their best work for both soil and plants.

Primroses (*Primula* species and hybrids), *Heuchera* and other spring-bloomers that send out new plants a month or so after blooming, should be separated when the new growth is large enough to be handled. In the case of *Heuchera,* which continues to bloom in good soil all summer, this might not be until September, still allowing time for the plants to get established before cold weather. Wild flowers like Dutchman's Breeches and other perennials, whose foliage dies down in summer, should be separated or moved shortly after bloom-ing, while you can still tell where they are. Most perennials of this nature are best planted where they are to remain and left to improve with the years.

Until you know your plants, dig and divide clumps with care. Some roots are tough and will stand almost anything; others, like those of False Bleeding Heart are brittle, and break off when least expected. Still others (*Tradescantia, Hemerocallis,* etc.) become so quickly interwoven it is almost impossible to separate them. Fortunately, these do not need frequent division although they profit by being divided every 4–5 years.

After disentangling, or chopping apart the roots of your spring-blooming perennials, keep them in soil or water until they are set into the ground. No roots should be allowed to dry out if you want the plant to grow. Soak them thoroughly if they seem dry. Plant according to directions, and with sev-eral inches of compost and soil between each plant.

Before planting spring-blooming perennials, learn as much about them as possible — read articles, look them up in garden encyclopedias, and talk to friends who have grown them. Learn before you plant that Sweet Rocket, though delightfully fragrant and a boon to the carefree gardener, is likely to take over an area if you allow it. Learn before you plant that the Christmas-Rose is temperamental and resents being moved once it is established. Learn before you plant that garden phlox grows tall and should reign at the back of the border, whereas wild Blue Phlox is scarcely more than a ground-cover except when it puts on its show of blue flower-clusters in spring.

What happens if you don't find out these things before you plant? Nothing at all, except that you learn by experience — "the hard way." Perhaps you're one of those people who prefers to learn that way, who think it's more fun to try things the experts *don't* recommend. Who knows — maybe it is!

OTHER SPRING PERENNIALS THAT LIKE SHADE

Adonis amurensis. Bright, buttercup-like flower with a collar of lacy green. Very early. Does best in partial shade; light, sandy humusy soil. Delightful. Foliage dies down in summer. Other varieties hard to find.

Amsonia tabernaemontana — Willow Amsonia. 2–3′. Purplish blue flowers in cymes, June–July. Attractive Milkweed pods. Rich soil, light and half shade.

Anchusa italica azurea — Italian Bugloss. 3–5′. Purple — dark blue — bright blue flowers. Do not allow to go to seed. Cut back after flowering. Likes to remain where planted in light to half shade.

Anemone sylvestris. To 12″. Nodding white flower. Handsome and hardy. Partial shade. Likes lime. *A. Pulsatilla* can be tried in light shade, in alkaline soil. Fairly heavy soil with good drainage.

Aquilegia — Columbine. 1–2′. Beautiful long-spurred varieties. Require rich light soil with bone meal and rotted manure. Protection from wind in light shade. Seedlings hardier and many times just as attractive as hybrids.

Arenaria montana — Mountain Sandwort. Flat mats of green with snow-white flowers. Must have sandy soil with good drainage. Light- and half-shade. Alpine and rock gardens.

Aruncus sylvester — Goats-Beard. Tall, background plant. Handsome, divided foliage. Flowers, white, in terminal panicles. Half-shade. Likes moist soil. Apt to be weedy except in right places.

Asperula odorata — Sweet Woodruff. 8″. Leaves in whorls. Prolific white blossoms in early spring. Lots of humus to hold the moisture. Can be used as a ground-cover or around rocks.

Aubrietia — Purple Rock-Cress. To 12″. More or less evergreen trailer with a mat of reddish purple flowers. Sun or light shade. Likes rocks.

Bellis perennis — English Daisy. Low, mat-like. Pink, white, red flowers. Blooms April–May, but continues in cool regions all summer. Partial shade in rich soil. Keep in coldframe over winter.

Bellium — Like a miniature English Daisy. Leaves in crowded rosettes. Tiny white daisy flowers. Agreeable to being moved any time anywhere, but keep over in coldframe.

Bergenia — Often listed as *Saxifraga or Megasea*. To 1′. Large rounded leaves almost evergreen. Bold pink or white flowers in early spring. Good for accents and among rocks. Any good soil.

Brunnera macrophylla or *Anchusa myosotidiflora* — Siberian Bugloss. 1½–2′. Heart-shaped leaves and Forget-Me-Not blue flowers. Prefers half- and light-shade. Needs moisture. Likes leaf mulch. Useful.

Campanula persicifolia — Peach-leaf *Campanula,* or Bell-flower. Leaf mat with stalks of flowers in spring and spasmodically all summer. Blue or white. Light shade. *C. Portenschlagiana* — trailing with quantities of soft blue flowers. Stony soil, plenty of humus, half-shade.

Delphinium tricorne — Rock larkspur. To 1'. Leaves, 3–5 parted. Blue flowers. May. Best around rocks. Foliage dies in summer.

Dicentra eximia — Wild Bleeding Heart. To 1'. Pretty lacy foliage. Sprays of "bleeding-heart-like" flowers. If happy, will bloom all summer. Temperamental. Likes rocks, part- to half-shade. *D. formosa.* Western Bleeding Heart. Similar to *D. eximia.*

Dicentra spectabilis — Bleeding Heart. To 2'. Sprays more graceful than former; flowers more like lines of hearts. Beautiful and graceful. Also likes the protection of rocks in light shade. Foliage usually dies.

Doronicum caucasicum — Caucasian Leopards-bane. To 2'. Leaves coarsely toothed, slightly heart-shaped. Yellow, daisy-like flowers. Half-shade. Rich loam, plenty of humus. Also *D. plantagineum* to 5'.

Epimedium macranthum or *grandiflorum* — One of daintiest, loveliest of spring blooms. Early airy racemes of rosy red, white, or yellow flowers. Stems of beautiful leaves edged with red develop to about 1 foot after blossoms die. Almost evergreen. Protect with pine boughs or plant in protected place. Loves woodsy humus and moisture. Other species to try.

Filipendula hexapetala — Drop-Wort. Ferny foliage excellent for edging. Sprays of delicate creamy white flowers rising well above leaves in May. Will tolerate light shade but must have air.

Haberlea rhodopensis — Low, dainty, tufted perennial with Gloxinia-like blossoms, blue to lilac. Choice alpine, liking rocks and crevices. Might need winter protection, but likes it cool in summer. *H. virginale,* beautiful white variety.

Day-Lilies start blooming in spring
and continue through summer.

Hemerocallis — Day-Lily. No garden is complete, without Day-Lilies. They take sun, light and deeper shade. At their best in light or part shade with plenty of air. Grow practically anywhere but love humus. Good for difficult banks. Fountain of grass-like foliage. Stalks of lily-like flowers rising from 2–4′ from leaves. Varieties start their blooming season in May with Lemon Lily *(H. flava)*, pale lovely yellow. Many other early varieties.

Hesperis matronalis — Sweet Rocket. 1–3′. Fragrant, old-fashioned flower, easily grown at the back of spring plantings. Lavendar or white pyramidal spikes of bloom are attractive and showy. Grows almost anywhere, but is not too weedy.

Heuchera sanguinea — Coral-Bells. Good edging plant with foliage to 1′. Attractive leaves. Flower stalks to 2′, with panicles of coral-colored flowers that last all summer if given plenty of humus and partial shade. Most desirable.

Hydrastis canadensis — Goldenseal. Orange-Root. To 1′. Grown principally for its beautiful lobed-leaves and raspberry-like fruits. Rich, moist soil in partial or light shade.

Iberis sempervirens — Evergreen Candytuft. 8–12″. White flowers in raceme-like heads. Likes sun but tolerates shade. Other varieties tried for results. Must have good drainage. Likes rocky soil.

Iris Siberica — Siberian Iris. Grass-like foliage in good clumps to 2′. Slender, graceful Iris flowers in white and blue shades, blooming almost in deep shade, but liking air-circulation. Grows in poor soil, but likes humus. Lovely beside a pool, or anywhere. *I. Pseudacorus.* Yellow Flag Iris. *I. cristata* — takes almost deep shade. See Chapter 2.

Lamium maculatum — Dead Nettle. To 1′. Variegated variety most attractive for shady gardens. Orchid blossoms. Makes good low focal point in shady plantings. *L. alba,* white.

Lathyrus vernus — Spring Bitter Vetch. 1–1½′. Flowers blue-violet, rose-pink, or white. March–May. Best in partial shade and tolerates quite a dense shade. Should be used more.

Lychnis Viscaria — German Catchfly. Prolific bloomer in sun and will tolerate light shade if there is enough air. Grassy leaves in tufts, which make good border plants. Stalks of flowers — a bright purply rose.

Omphalodes cappadocia or *cornifolia* — Navelwort. 9″. Stout clumps. Sprays of brilliant blue Forget-Me-Not flowers. Easy to grow but need moisture. Likes rock gardens and pools. Grows in deep shade but blooms better in light shade. *O. verna,* trailing.

Paeonia — Peony. Sometimes sold for shady places, but takes only very light shade or partial shade. Roots must have plenty of room and rich soil (manure and compost). Stems will grow toward the sun. But under high trees they do very well on 5–6 hours of sun a day and are excellent "filler" plants.

Pentstemon — Beardtongue. Thrives best in open situation but takes partial shade, particularly in warm climates. Lovely blue species in California. Likes moist soil, but well-drained.

Petasites fragrans — Winter Heliotrope. 10″. Blooms in winter or early spring; blue-purple; delightful odor. Large bold leaves good contrast in summer shady garden.

Phlox divaricata — Wild Blue Phlox. 9–18″ while in bloom (several weeks). Lovely Phlox stalks of blue. Excellent in wild garden or perennial border. Likes humus.

Polemonium caeruleum — Jacobs-Ladder. 1½–3′. Finely cut foliage like fern fronds. Pretty blue flowers. Sun or light shade. Plenty of humus in soil. *P. repens* — Called "Creeping Polemonium," but is actually the Jacobs-Ladder of many gardens and does not "creep." It is a low clump to 1′.

Primula — Primrose. Varieties too numerous to mention. Most are fine for the semi-shaded garden. Likes it cool and plenty of humus and moisture in the soil. Leafmold tucked under leaves in fall is good. Lovely yellows, white, pink, etc.

Pulmonaria officinalis — Lungwort. To 1½′. Clump of basal leaves, splotched and marked with lighter green — most decorative. Pinkish blue flowers, somewhat like those of *Mertensia.*

Plants remain lush and beautiful all summer in shade with plenty of leafmold compost. *P. saccharata* and *P. augusti-folia,* and others.

Ramonda. Choice alpines for rock gardens. Rosette of crinkly leaves. Bell-shaped flowers, violet-purple. Rock crevices in acid, peaty soil, in shade. Good drainage. Hard to establish.

Ranunculus—Buttercup. Native Buttercups will often appear in a woodsy garden, particularly if it is swampy. Several allied species (*R. montanus*) do well in partial shade, but must be ferreted out. Most need winter protection in the North. *R. ficaria.* Low, mounded foliage, glistening yellow flowers.

Saxifraga decipiens — Crimson Moss. Mossy plant to 1'. White flowers May-June. Foliage turns beautiful crimson as winter approaches. Watch for other species and varieties.

Silene virginica — Fire Pink. To 2'. Scarlet or crimson flowers with notched petals. From May throughout summer. Wild garden or border. Light shade.

Soldanella alpina. To 6". Natives of the Alps. Roundish leaves. Umbels of pale blue flowers. Moist shade among rocks. *S. montana.* Fringed lavender blossoms. Larger than preceding.

Synthyris. Charming rock-garden plant. Neat rosettes of leathery leaves. Spikes of showy flowers, blue and violet. Acid soil, rich in humus; partial shade.

Thalictrum aquilegifolium — Columbine Meadow-Rue. To 3½'. Rosy purple clustered flowers. May-July. Likes humus and moisture. Only light shade. *T. dioicum;* native plant to 2'. Dry woodland.

Tradescantia — Spiderwort. Will flourish in almost any soil, sun, or light shade. Some of the newer varieties are pretty, but all grow very easily and can become weedy.

Trollius — Globe-Flower. Globe-shaped flowers in yellow and orange. Swampy conditions, but adapt themselves in good garden soil with plenty of humus. Several varieties; bloom May-August.

Viola — Garden Viola, developed from *V. cornuta* with many lovely varieties. Grows easily but enjoys rich soil and shelter from hot sun. *V. odorata* — the Sweet Violet from Europe likes partial shade in humusy soil. Delightfully fragrant. Several colors.

Vancouveria — American Barrenwort. Closely related to *Epimedium*. Attractive in the rock garden or ground-cover for the wild garden. Compound leaves. Rather small white flowers. Light to full shade. Rich soil.

4

Shade-Tolerant Perennials for Summer and Fall

✦❋✦❀✦❋✦❀✦❋✦❀✦❋✦❀✦❋✦❀✦❋✦❀✦❋✦❀✦❋✦❀✦❋✦❀✦❋✦❀✦

IN SUMMER the shady gardener has an advantage over the gardener in the sun. The shade is cool and inviting. Not so many weeds flaunt their unwelcome seed pods. There's something encouraging about a summer garden in the shade: if plants have had any care at all, they seem pert and fresher; the flowers are brighter; the leaves don't surrender to dejection.

True, there is not the rampant color brandished by sunloving annuals, but there are a number of plants that are worth considering for summer blossoms in the shade. A number of these are merely shade-tolerant. Their foliage is good and the flowers fewer than with more sun, but those few are rich and deep in color, sometimes larger and more perfect. Other plants actually prefer the shade and, if treated well, will continue year after year to brighten up shady corners with satisfying regularity.

Although June 21 officially begins summer, some hot-weather blossoms arrive before that. *Heuchera,* for example, first rings its coral bells in May, but all summer new bells play stand-ins for the old until September, when stalks are bare and must be broken off. Feathery, rosy purple clusters of *Thalictrum aquilegifolium* bloom before the summer solstice, other varieties carrying on through July and August with yellow and creamy white blossoms. False Bleeding Heart (*Dicentra eximia*) blooms in spring too. It continues for two months into the summer, but I have found it temperamental, pouting near other wild flowers where it was installed because of similar requirements, and proffering luxuriant sprays of flowers and foliage in front of a shady shrubbery border where it had arrived by accident.

With no time for garden prima donnas, the gardener of difficult shady places will welcome a member of the Lily Family, *Hemerocallis.* Crisp apricot, tawny oranges, cheery yellows are his partners here, to lighten garden-gloom. There'll be tall stalks of exquisitely-formed Day-Lilies, so called because the individual flowers bloom only for a single day. But, with the closing of one, another is ready to open, so that you are unaware of the pause in bloom. With the right choice of varieties, the *Hemerocallis*-grower can begin the season with the fragrant Lemon-Lily, enjoy at least one variety in bloom through the rest of the spring and summer, close it with Autumn Prince or Yellow Frills. Poor soil, dry, shady banks, rocky hillsides, bright sun, woodsy shade — it's all the same to some of the vigorous varieties. They'll grow and bloom anywhere. They appreciate compost, however, and a few of the more delicate types need better conditions to be at their best, but they're all remarkably tolerant.

At the edge of our driveway, we have a row, on the top

of a sharp, shady incline. The snow piles high in winter, and
the best soil is washed down the slope in spring rains, leaving
the Day-Lilies in a bed of sandy subsoil mulched with small
driveway-stones. Undaunted, their pointed green shoots push
through the hard earth every spring, to develop into a fountain of foliage — long thin blades that remain green all
summer.

Given compost, manure, and a little attention now and
then, they respond gloriously — flower stalks to 4 feet sometimes, with twice as many blossoms (under a little sun), and
with large firm flower petals. With their Northern winter
hardiness, their staunch endurance of Southern heat as far
down as Southern Florida, and their good-natured tolerance
of so many other conditions, they have much to recommend
them to the gardener-in-the-shade.

Many summer perennials which grow in the shade are
actually wild flowers. A dried-up swamp at the edge of a woodland is their favorite haunt, or the bank of a brook just before
it winds into the woods. Have you never seen there, the clusters of white or pink turtle-head flowers at the top of a stem?
Chelone, the plant is called, after the Greek for tortoise or
turtle. Neglected in the wilds, yet given a choice place in the
shady garden where it will not be too dry, it becomes an
intriguing oddity to build up interest in the summer garden.

Perhaps you have happened across the pert, bright bracts
of *Monarda didyma,* a showy flower dressed in scarlet, pink,
white, or red for garden use. You will like large colonies of the
red variety planted next to white Phlox under high Oak
branches, or the soft glow of the pink splashed across the
prickly face of a Blue Spruce, or a colony of white set against
White Pine to bring out the shadows.

The Campanulas, refined of flower and foliage, have a cultivated look about them, even though many of them have not yet been tamed. Some wedge their roots in rocky crevices; others prefer the banks of streams. At least one species goes creeping about in waste places, and in the corners of the garden reserved for weeds. *Campanula rapunculoides,* or Creeping Bellflower, often seems to appear from nowhere, until suddenly — in August — there are lavender bells clinging to one side of a tall stalk. They are certainly an answer to the gardener in the shade who wants summer bloom. The plant will grow practically anywhere, in sun or shade, waste places or good garden soil, dressing up a neglected corner, surrendering without a struggle should it not be wanted.

Nothing could be more striking in its stately dignity than the clear beautiful red of the Cardinal Flower *(Lobelia cardinalis)*, a spire of colorful blossoms on majestic 4'-stalks. Some wild flower enthusiasts think it should not be transported from its native habitat — pine and red maple woodland at the edges of, or in, a swamp. But all too often these are the very places that are filled in and used for building sites, and choice wild plants are buried forever.

Here is opportunity for the gardener-in-the-shade. Whether or not you have a recognized wild-flower garden, build up a spot under trees with well-rotted woodsy humus, preferably against the low branches of Pine trees, and let it be your Cardinal Flower retreat. If you have a spot beside a pool or a stream, so much the better, but don't let the lack of anything but trees keep you from adding this colorful summer beauty to your garden.

The other hardy Lobelia *(L. syphilitica)* is not quite so striking; but it, too, is an excellent shady-garden subject. Many a bit of dying bulb-foliage can be hidden behind its full-leaved stalks as it grows to maturity. Come late summer, the 2'-spires are splashed with vivid blue, a pretty companion for pale pink houseplant Begonias.

A stretch of woodland or woodsy marshland at your shovel's tip is to be envied by the adventurous gardener. For there is where you can grow hazy purple masses of Joe-Pye-Weed (*Eupatorium purpureum*) and the massed white blossom-heads of *E. urticaefolium*, or White Snakeroot. The latter is attractive in a large area where it can grow to its full 4'. A third relative harmonizes with some of the early pink Chrysanthemums; this is *E. coelestinum*, with fuzzy round lavender buttons of flowers like annual Ageratum.

Growing in the wild, Eupatoriums are lost in the heat and confusion of late summer. "Weedy things," we think as we snub their hairy foliage. Also we overlook the beauty of Golden Rod, Queen Anne's Lace, Mountain Asters, Steeplebush, Meadow-sweet, and other native flowers. Yet these blossoms will grow under the trees in gardens; and given care and placed where they'll show to advantage, they supply needed bloom into the fall.

Most people coming upon *Phlox paniculata* and *P. maculata* growing in light woodland consider them escaped garden flowers instead of the wild species from which our present garden varieties have been developed. They are like inferior garden blooms, rather scrawny, with dull magenta florets. We want showy masses, particularly for gardens in the shade. And we find them in a few of our summer-blooming shady plants, notably Phlox. From years of cultivation and hybridization have emerged some beautiful varieties in brilliant hues, of which Sir John Falstaff is one of the newer ones. The large salmon-pink florets unfold in almost continuous bloom from July into September.

Most varieties of Phlox will take light shade and partial shade. A few can stand quite a dense shade providing they grow where they have room and good air-circulation. Separated every two years (instead of the usual three to four) and given ample compost, the stems grow tall, but straight, the blossom panicles deeper in color and quite respectable in size.

Making a prolific display in swamps and meadows is Purple Loosestrife (*Lythrum Salicaria*). Like the common Daisy, *Hemerocallis fulva,* and some of the Campanulas, it is an immigrant that apparently likes our country. We now have several varieties of garden *Lythrum,* the best to date being Morden's Pink. It is not a dramatic flower, but its continuous blossoms, of a good rose, are a welcome innovation to sparse July bloom. In part shade (four to five hours of sun a day) its leaves are glossier and greener, the flowers deeper in color; whereas in full sunlight the foliage is poor and the spikes of flowers more numerous but not individually so lovely.

In nature many summer-blooming plants are commandingly tall. Most of them (Phlox, *Aconitum,* etc.) should be used toward the back of a flower border. Such a spot is in my own garden, with *Aconitum* almost directly under some Dogwood trees. In front are several clumps of Iris that bloom in spite of the shade, against the glossy deep-green of the Monkshood. To complete this garden-picture is *Hosta viridis marginata,* a round footstool of chartreuse, with individual leaves edged in olive. We now have three heights, stepped down in an interesting manner, contrasting in form and foliage, each with a different period of bloom, and each satisfied with its share of sunlight.

In a garden splashed with shade, there are apt to be flower beds of a different type than the traditional perennial border.

Perennials are mixed in with the foundation shrubs. There might be flower beds around trees; or trees, shrubs, and perennials arranged in dramatic garden-pictures. Or there might simply be bold masses of flowers against the green of pines or other shrubby growth.

In my garden, where White Pines are abundant, a particular spot called for high-growing showy flowers that could be enjoyed from a distance. White Phlox with a pink eye was the answer. Next to it was planted a colony of deep Pink Phlox. During July and August they are prominent masses of pink and white against the green.

In front of another pine-needled back-drop, Queen-of-the-Meadows (*Filipendula Ulmaria*) takes the stage with dense creamy white racemes in July. These tall summer perennials are used as single displays, and stand not too near their backgrounds: each clump a good 4–5 feet from the other, and 5–8 feet from the lower Pine branches. Not in conventional patterns, they have been adapted to the long range garden-picture. Tall, they serve also as transition plants, bringing together the woodsy background of the garden-in-general and the more formalized area of the garden-proper. They receive from four to six hours of direct sunlight a day plus a few odd-hours of spattered sunlight and light shade.

It is difficult to determine how much sun or shade any plant receives; the amount of sunlight varies, not only in hours, but from day to day. What plants best take changing conditions? Would Pink Turtlehead be happier under the Oaks where it will find less sun but more moisture? Should Mist-flower be moved from under the Dogwood, whose branches reach almost to smothering level? Would Foxglove thrive better where the shade is denser but where the water drains more freely? The answers lie in experiments and observations. Learn to experiment with your shade and your plants. This book can only make suggestions; it cannot answer all your questions or tell you where your plants will thrive.

(Mass. Horticultural Soc.)

Shooting star *(Dodocatheon)* growing near azaleas.

Asters are among the tall summer and fall-blooming plants, but only two endure shade requirements; *Aster acuminatus,* or Whorled Aster, with snowy white flower heads at the top of a 2–3 foot stalk; and *Aster cordifolius,* with branching sprays of blue flowers. Whorled Aster tranquilly accepts a dense shade in dry, poor soil at times. Not tall enough to dignify a commanding position, it nevertheless makes an excellent filler, or transition plant between Monkshood and low Hostas, or Phlox and Coral Bells.

A. cordifolius can be used for similar purposes, preferring spots where more sunlight filters through the leaves, or where it can drink in a few hours of direct sunlight. Both species like the ease and comfort of cultivation.

Some Goldenrods will seed themselves in shaded areas and grow very well, although only one — the Wreath Goldenrod (*Solidago caesia*) — grows naturally in shade. Weedy, we might consider them as they luxuriate beside the road, but their warm yellow color is a welcome addition to shady gardens.

If you want to save trouble for yourself, move plants at the accepted time. If, however, you have a chance to acquire a plant you particularly desire, and it's the wrong time, take it and nurse it along rather than sacrifice the opportunity.

Separating summer-blooming perennials requires skill and heed to timing. In general, the time to separate any plant is after it has finished blooming. This means late summer for most summer-blooming perennials, though a few are better divided in spring, and often the choice is up to the gardener.

How often to separate? That usually depends on the gardener, the knowledge he has of his plant's habits — and how

(Paul E. Genereux)

Anemone sylvestris is a hardy late summer perennial.

lazy he is. Some plants bear separating every year and are better for it, like Phlox and Blue Lobelia. Usually, however, these and most summer perennials can go for at least two years and be none the worse, although the more compost and

Red *Monarda didyma* planted under high branches.

room their roots have when growing in the shade, the firmer, straighter stalks they will grow to support their flowers. The Peach-leaved Campanula increases the size of its leaf-mat every year, but the plants are weak and the blossom-stalks few unless they are separated every two to four years and given plenty of compost. *Hosta* and *Hemerocallis,* although thriving on humus, grow better after several years in the same place, entwining their roots, digging them deeper into the soil, the longer they stay. But neither *Hosta* nor *Hemerocallis* resents dividing. On the other hand, Christmas-Rose does. When once it is happily established it likes to stay put, and to have its family remain there too. Move or separate it only in emergencies.

If unfamiliar with certain plants we may suspect that they need separating, when:

1. Plant is not blooming well,
2. Blossoms are small and often malformed,
3. Too many lower leaves wither away,
4. Wilts easily,
5. Seems in general poor health.

When separating summer-blooming perennials allow from 5–12 inches between each plant, depending on the ultimate size of the plant and the root system. Dig up the clump and pull plants apart, treating each as an individual. Dig a hole wide and deep enough so that the roots can stretch to their full extent. Fill hole with water if ground is dry. Set in the plant with its neck level with the top of the ground. Work in good friable soil around the roots and press firmly. Between this plan and others turn in several trowelfuls of compost (depending on plant). Coarse compost loved by such plants as Phlox, Japanese Anemones, or *Monarda* can be chopped into the soil with a trowel, but always have sifted compost or friable loam around the roots of any plant.

While working with the individual plants, keep the rest of your clump covered with soil or the roots set in water. *Never* let the roots dry out. More plants are lost because of dry roots (either during or after planting) than for any other reason. When the new clump has been planted, and the hole filled about two-thirds with soil, water well, letting it soak in gently. Tamp the earth firmly about the roots, making sure that the neck of the plant is level with the ground. Cut off dead flower stalks, if any, and keep plants covered for several days, particularly during dry or sunny weather.

SHADE-TOLERANT PERENNIALS BLOOMING IN SUMMER AND FALL

Aconitum Napellus — Monkshood. Tall perennial blooming in July–September. Likes bone meal, wood ashes, and humusy soil in the shade and partial shade. Leaves, dark and shiny. Flowers, like blue helmets. Interesting. Roots poisonous; plant should not be grown near the vegetable garden. Otherwise, no danger in the average garden. Bi-color has blue and white helmets. Other late-blooming and taller species. Cool climate.

Androsace lanuginosa — Rock Jasmine. True alpines, growing above timber line. Difficult for average gardener. Shade. Gritty soil with good drainage. Trailing silky silver-green foliage. Rosy lilac flowers in late summer. A challenge!

Anemone japonica — Japanese Anemone. Flowers to 3′. Beautiful pinks and white. Several varieties. Lovely if they can be established. Like shade and much humus and rotted manure, moisture, good drainage.

Aster acuminatus — Whorled Aster. 1–3′. Leaves dark and bushy all summer; good, low filler-plant. Flower stalks branching to rather large flower head. Individual white flowers, 1″.

(*Gottscho-Schleisner*)

Astilbe brightens a stone wall in the shade of an old apple tree.

An excellent plant for waste shady places. Grows in poor soil, withstands drought. With better soil, grows luxuriantly. *A. cordifolius.* Blue Aster — needs lighter shade than preceding.

Astilbe. Various species used to develop lovely varieties. 1–6′. Most garden plants low. Foliage, attractive, compound, sometimes with reddish cast. Flowers, feathery plumes from white to deep pink. Excellent plant. Prefers shady places, but must have moisture; therefore, humus in soil to retain moisture. Mulch well in summer. If leaves dry, water soon revives them. Dried flower heads good for winter arrangements.

Baptisia leucantha. To 4′. Long spires of white flowers, June–July. Likes to grow in a clump and not be moved. Filler-plant. Any soil, but likes humus and light shade. *B. tinctoria,* Wild Indigo, can be used in the shade. *B. australis* — handsomest for garden use, will take very light shade.

Begonia evansiana — Hardy Begonia. Lobed, Begonia leaves and small flowers (pink). Should have pine-bough covering over winter. Good drainage. Humus. Low-growing.

Buphthalmum speciosum — to 2′. Recommended for sun, but will take part shade. Yellow daisy-like flowers in June and on. Bushy, compact growth.

Campanula persicifolia — Peach-leaved Campanula. Narrow leaves at base. Stalks of bell-shaped flowers in white and blue. June through summer. Numerous small new plants at base should be separated to keep plant's vigor. *C. carpatica* — wide, open bells of blue or white. *C. rapunculoides* — Creeping Bellflower. One-sided spikes of lavender-blue blossoms, really quite handsome. Will grow on dry hillsides in shade; the more sun, the better bloom, however. In good soil, grows lush and lovely. Other cultivated varieties.

Chelone glabra — White Turtle-Head. To 3′. Interesting white turtle-head flowers in late summer. Partial shade. Likes moisture and humus. *C. Lyoni* — Pink species.

Cimicifuga racemosa — Black Cohosh. To 8', in rich woodland soil. Segmented leaves attractive. Long spires of white blossoms most interesting. One of best late-bloomers. *C. simplex,* lower but just as handsome. Blooms in fall.

(Paul E. Genereux)

Colchicum blooms in the fall.

Coreopsis. 1–4'. Plant itself not much of an addition to a garden, but the yellow daisy-like flowers are bright and numerous. Likes sun, but will tolerate light shade, or as little as five to six hours of sun per day. Grows in poor soil. Good for barren bank.

Echinacea purpurea — Purple Coneflower. 3–5′. Large flower heads with prominent "cone" center, in purplish red, rose, or white. Tolerates light shade in rich, deep soil. Improves if left alone five to six years in a clump. Several good varieties, some probably crossed with *Rudbeckia* to which it is closely allied.

Eupatorium coelestinum — Mist-Flower. To 3′. Blue to violet flowers in delicate fluffy heads. Sun, or shade. Blooms last into fall. Lovely. *E. urticaefolium* — White Snakeroot. Massed heads of white flowers to 4′. Both good for garden interest. In natural areas at edge of woodlands. *E. purpureum* (Joe-Pye-Weed) and *E. perfoliatum* (Boneset) make good displays.

Filipendula Ulmaria — Queen of the Meadows. 2–6′. Good for background height, but not shrubby. Flowers, white, in rather dense paniculate cymes. A lovely thing. Try *F. camtschatica*. Might be sold as Spirea.

Gentiana Andrewsii — Closed Gentian. One of the most beautiful blue flowers. To 2′. Colonies establish well in wild garden for late summer bloom. Likes moisture and humus. *G. asclepiadea*. To 1½′. Grows easily in good soil.

Gillenia trifoliata. 2–3′. Flowers light rose or white. June–July. Graceful in growth. Grows easily in any good soil, preferring partial shade.

Helleborus niger — Christmas-Rose. Evergreen, palmately divided leaves. White to pinkish flowers in winter and very early spring. Likes shade and protection from wind. Enjoys humus and rotted manure — and plenty. Blooms prolifically when once established where it is happy. *H. orientalis* — Lenten-Rose. White to various shades of purple. Similar requirements of preceding.

Hemerocallis — Day-Lily. Many varieties blooming through summer. (See Chapter 3 — Page 46)

Heuchera — Coral Bells. Blooms through summer. See Chapter 3.

Hosta — Plaintain Lily. All the varieties have blossoms (white and varying shades of blue and purple); some of them attractive. But the genus as a group is so much more important for foliage effects that it is listed in Chapter 8.

Jasione perennis — Sheeps-Bit. Low. For edging or rock gardens. Tufted rosettes of oblong leaves. Globular heads of blue flowers. June to July. Ordinary soil in sun or partial shade. *J. humilis.*

Lathyrus latifolius — Perennial Pea. 4–8', in a twiney growth. Can be trained to trellises or over walls. Hardy and easy to grow, in loose, humusy soil. Prefers partial shade; sometimes a deep shade. Pink to red pea-like flowers. *L. vernus,* rose-pink or white; *L. luteus,* yellow to orange.

Ligularia clivorum (*Senecio*) — Bigleaf Goldenray. Stately plants. Large yellow daisy-like flowers on 4–5' stems. Hardy to New York, but try as far north as Boston in protected place. Rich, deep soil; plenty of humus and manure. Likes shade.

Lobelia cardinalis — Cardinal-Flower. To 4'. Narrow leaves and a spire of lovely red blossoms. Likes the shallow waters of slowly moving streams and the shade of nearby trees. Will establish in a shady garden with plenty of humus so the moisture is retained; also some extra watering. *L. siphilitica.* With a spire of blossoms as brilliant a blue as the former is red. To 3'. Bushier foliage; a good filler-plant for the mid-shady border. Grows best when divided every year or so, in early spring.

Lysimachia clethroides. To 3'. White flowers in attractive spikes. Foliage good through summer. Attractive fall coloring. Naturally moisture-loving, so needs plenty of humus in the soil.

Lythrum Salicaria — Purple Loosestrife. 2–3'. Rather spindly plant with purply flowers in a spike. Blooms for weeks through the summer. Var. Morden's Pink an excellent improvement in both color (more of a rose) and growth. Sun and moisture-loving, but takes to the garden. Will get along with five to six hours of sun and partial shade with glossier foliage and lovelier flowers.

Meconopsis cambrica — Welsh-Poppy. To 1½'. Rosettes of gray-green leaves. Charming crinkled poppies of red and orange. Must have cool in summer and rich sandy loam in light shade. Needs shelter from winds and winter protection. Difficult.

Monarda didyma — Bee-Balm. To 3'. Odd flowers surrounded by matching bracts in scarlet, white, red, pink. Square stems and aroma of Mint Family. Delightful. Easily grown even in poor soil. Prefers partial shade and appreciates humus. Bees appreciate it. *M. fistulosa* — Wild Bergamot. Lavender and lilac blossoms. Likes more sun but grows easily. Not so lovely as preceding.

Oenothera linearis — Sun-Drops. Bright yellow flowers a needed spot in the shady garden. Slender leaves, reddish in fall. Actually a sun-loving plant, but does well in shade though not so robust or prolific of bloom. Give extra humus and air.

Parnassia — Grass of Parnassus. Dainty wild flower blooming in late summer. White blossom. Low. Moisture. Part shade.

Phlox paniculata — Garden Phlox. To 6'. Strong-growing. Makes good background plant. Lower varieties, good filler plants. Several good whites. Lovely salmons, and pinks, and other red tones. Easily grown. In shade; give extra humus to keep stems sturdy. Delicate fragrance.

Physalis Alkekengi — Chinese Lantern. Grow only in waste places where this can take over. Flowers inconspicuous, but large tomato-red "lanterns," used for winter decorations, are beautiful.

Physostegia — False Dragonhead. To 3'. Sturdy spikes of pinkish blossoms like miniature "dragon heads." Will overrun if care is not used. Takes very light shade.

Platycodon grandiflorum — Balloon-Flower. Blue and white balloon-like flowers. Interesting. Will tolerate light shade, but give extra humus and water.

Prunella vulgaris — Heal-All. Old-world herb, now wild. In a clump to 1′, this makes a good addition to the shady garden. Flowers, lavender. Grows easily.

Rudbeckia laciniata — Golden-Glow. 5–8′. Good background plant for large group of plants, or as bold picture against trees. Double yellow blossoms. Prefers sun, but will tolerate some shade. Likes rich well-drained soil. Red aphis bothersome.

Sanguisorba minor — Burnet. Grows in pretty, low, sprawly clumps to 10″. Purple flowers in July. Tender leaves used for salads.

Saponaria officinalis — Bouncing Bet. 1½–2½′. A cheery pretty plant with large rose-tinged flowers. Originally from England, it has now taken over fields and waysides, but it grows well in lightly shaded waste places. Don't let it take over a cultivated area.

Saxifraga umbrosa — London Pride. To 1′. For rock garden or the front of the border. Dark green foliage; sprays of pinkish flowers. Like shade from summer sun.

Solidago caesia — Wreath Goldenrod. To 2′. Semi-shade. Aug. to Oct. Weedy in rich soil, but usually neat and well behaved in shade. A bright spot.

Spigelia marilandica — Pink-Root. To 2′. June to July. Red, tubular flowers. Likes light shade and good loam.

Tanacetum vulgare — Tansy. To 3′. An escaped Old-World plant, growing in all kinds of waste places. But its late summer yellow bloom is welcome in the shady garden. Grows in any soil. Attractive foliage.

Thalictrum dipterocarpum — Meadow-Rue. To 2′. Lilac flowers in August. Handsome. Loamy soil. Light shade.

Tradescantia virginiana — Spiderwort. From this species most of the new hybrids have been born. Strong growers and will tolerate light shade. Blue and purple tones. Blooms throughout summer.

Valeriana offinalis — Garden-Heliotrope. Rather sparse stalks 4–5′. Numerous flowers in whitish, pinkish, or lavender heads. Scents up the whole garden. Will tolerate light shade but needs air-circulation. Inclines to being weedy.

5

Annuals and Biennials That Bloom in Shade

✧❀✧❀✧❀✧❀✧❀✧❀✧❀✧❀✧❀✧❀✧❀✧❀✧❀✧

ANNUALS ARE PLANTS that grow, bloom, go to seed, and die in a single season. Keep the flowers picked so that the plants will not produce seeds and stop blooming. The result is color, gayety, profusion well into fall.

Many seeds of annuals are large, easy to see, and easy for the amateur to grow. Zinnias and Marigolds, which are sunloving but which bloom sparsely in the shade, fall into this category. Other seeds, such as Petunias, are minute and difficult for most people to handle. The new hybrid Petunias do not germinate readily and most gardeners find it more convenient to buy small plants from local growers.

As a rule annuals are sun-loving plants. Yet there are a few which enjoy, or at least tolerate, a light shade. Others will endure shade and give sparse bloom if they have an abundance of the other necessary requisites — plenty of water, rich soil, and good air-circulation.

With the tendency toward smaller homes and yards, and the scarcity of labor, spacious cutting-gardens are seldom seen any more. There is no room for row after row of annuals, and no time to cut them. Flowers in quantity are confined to the vegetable garden, small groups are distributed among perennials to lend color and to fill in where perennials need replacing.

As a rule this mixing of annuals and perennials works out very well, especially if the annuals are planted near early bloomers such as Iris, *Baptisia,* Tulips, and *Hemerocallis.* Phlox, and other tall-growing perennials, whose lower leaves are apt to dry up can be greatly benefited by bushy annuals settling at their feet. Use Sweet Alyssum or annual Lobelia, which have prolific mounds of blossoms.

Ageratum, with blossom-buttons of lavender or white is another annual with which to clothe undressed places. One of the best for lightly shaded areas, it is ideal for porch or window boxes, for carpeting bare spots, or bordering a perennial bed in light shade. Seeds germinate readily when the ground is warm, but if you want immediate effect, buy small plants. By summer's end two dozen set 12–15″ apart will have edged a plot 24′ long.

The nice thing about annuals, particularly in a garden which is not weeded too meticulously, is that seedlings often appear to replace old plants. Love-in-a-Mist *(Nigella)* comes up all over the place, parents, children, and grandchildren together. The plants like sun but often fall in shady spots, filling them with ferny foliage and an abundance of sky-blue lacy flowers. Even the seed pods are decorative — fat light tan globes for a light touch in your flower arrangements.

Behind something shrubby tuck in a few *Nicotiana* plants, and stake to prevent their sprawling, then sniff what they do to your shaded garden. They are worth planting just for their fragrance, and will come up another year. Self-sown seedlings of Petunias tolerate more shade than you might think, and bloom in spite of it.

Whereas an annual grows and blossoms in the same season, a biennial comes up the first season but usually takes two years to bloom. Since there are only a few biennials that tolerate shade we are including them with the annuals.

The tall spires of old-fashioned Foxglove (*Digitalis purpurea*) do something for the silhouette of a shady garden. The white or rosy purple thimble-flowers give life to the shadows at a time when other bloom is scarce. But they're tricky. They must have good drainage and protection, particularly over their first winter. They like an abundance of compost in the soil. The seeds germinate in July and for weeks there are unnoticed colonies of downy leaves which grow to large rosettes before freezing time. In early spring they mark time, until suddenly in May spires of buds start growing sometimes to 7'. If there is a question about wintering the young plants, place them in a cold frame, or tuck in additional compost around the leaves and cover with a basket or large glass bowl.

Honesty is another favorite biennial. Sometimes it acts like an annual and will bloom the first season if planted early enough. In northern gardens, plant the seeds during the summer in a neglected spot, leaving it un-mulched until the new plants are well established. The following spring there will be branching spires of 4-petaled orchid-colored flowers. During the summer the flat brown seed pods are not very handsome, but rub off the outside coverings, let the seeds fall where they may, and you have remaining whole bou-

(Paul E. Genereux)

Tall Foxgloves add to the silhouette of
a garden and give life to the shadows.

quets of "silver pennies" which you can use for winter
flower arrangements.

Where do Forget-Me-Nots fit into the botanical categories? Are they annuals, biennials, or perennials? Catalogues
list them as all three. Mine I've acquired from friends. Some

plants live from year to year, others for a year or two, and then die. All of them produce hordes of yellow-eyed children dressed in rich sky-blue — appealing waifs that bloom for weeks. Their progeny are moved in the fall to make spring borders for various gardens, leaving others to fill in the shady rock garden.

The Viola Family is another in which there are annuals, biennials, and perennials. Johnny-Jump-Ups (*V. tricolor*) pop up and bloom (preferably in sun) the first season, spring, summer, and fall. Violets are perennials, needing two seasons in order to bloom. Pansies are treated as annuals in the North, but are actually biennials that often live over a third and fourth season. Violas are similar. Almost all members of the family have a winsome appeal. Empty indeed is the garden without them.

In planting, biennials and annuals are treated similarly. It is not necessary to divide plants every few years as it is with perennials. There is only the lifting and transplanting of small new plants, and the setting out of nursery-bought plants in the spring.

Prepare the soil ahead of time. If the space to be filled is large, work in plenty of rotted manure or compost. Chop and rake the soil to make it smooth. At planting time dig a hole large enough to encompass the plant with a generous ball of earth. Disturb the roots as little as possible. Set in plant, firming the soil so that it is well anchored. Water well if soil is dry. Keep plants covered with flower pots, berry boxes, etc., from one to seven days depending on weather and types of plants.

In setting out small seedlings directly from a seedbed, do not expose roots to the air. Dig the hole deep enough

(Paul E. Genereux)

Yellow-eyed, pink and white Forget-Me-Nots make colorful borders for shady gardens.

to take care of their entire length and press sifted earth gently around them. Keep covered until the plant can withstand conditions without wilting.

If your planting space is small — among perennials or in front of shrubs, etc. — prepare the soil by hand. Turn it over with a trowel (not difficult in a well-tended garden) before setting in your plants. Smooth over the planted area with a scratcher. If the weather is very dry, leave a miniature moat around each plant to catch extra water so it can soak in around the roots instead of running off.

In growing annuals from seed, they are divided into three groups: hardy annuals, sown in fall or early spring to bloom from midsummer to fall; semi-hardy, sown in a flat or cold-frame (in the North) for extra start, or out of doors when the ground is warm; and tender annuals sown very early indoors (January-March) if their blossoms are to be enjoyed before frost.

Catalogues and directions which come with seeds give specific information, often including the hardiness of a plant and the time it takes to germinate. This is based on average climates and must be tempered with your experience and that of others in your vicinity. In the South and some parts of the West, the excessive heat, not the cold, is the problem. In such places hardy annuals are sown in fall and winter, and blossoms enjoyed through the spring. Tender annuals (usually sun-loving) carry the southern gardener through the hot weather.

Most annuals that bloom in the shade fall into the hardy category. These usually germinate more quickly and grow better when the seeds are sown on open ground in fall or spring. Many of them resent transplanting, such as *Nigella* and Sweet Alyssum.

(George C. Robbins)

Love-in-a-Mist fills shady spots with
ferny foliage and sky-blue flowers.

Every gardener has his own method of starting seeds.
Some have a hotbed; others, a coldframe. Some use a greenhouse or pit. Except in a large bay window, where the seedlings can receive uniform light and greater humidity, con-

ditions in a house tend to make seedlings spindling. But seeds are often started in the cellar, in flats, and set into a hotbed or coldframe.

Since I have no greenhouse, I start seeds indoors (in the spring) usually in wooden flats, frequently in large flower pots, and sometimes in coffee cans with holes punched about 1″ from the bottom for drainage. The important things are the proper inducements to seed-germination — warmth and moisture. Seeds do not need light to germinate. Indeed, many people place something over the top to keep out the light. I set my seed containers in a darkish place with a piece of glass over the top.

Flats, or seed boxes can be had in various sizes. For ease of handling I like them approximately 7 by 14″ and 4″ high. But I use what I have on hand, which have been acquired through the years by purchasing nursery-grown plants. You probably will do the same and may find my directions helpful until you work out your own method.

Place a layer of stones and broken crockery at the bottom for drainage, then a layer of sphagnum or coarse peat moss over the stones so the soil won't wash through. Fill to within one inch of the top with a sifted mixture consisting of one-half good loam, one-fourth decomposed compost with a little manure added, and one-fourth sand. (Seeds germinate better in a soil that is not too rich.) Spread soil evenly and firm with a brick or small board. Cover with a thin layer of commercial mica. Plant seeds according to directions. Cover with another layer of mica. Set container in water until soil becomes evenly moist.

Mica for use in planting is sold in a number of popular brands. These have been especially prepared and treated so that they are good sterile materials to aid in seed planting; they do not dry out so quickly as soil and sand, but hold the moisture evenly, and hasten germination. They also discourage the "damping off" of young seedlings.

Set planted seed-flats in a temperature of about 60° and place a piece of glass over the top for further humidity. Care should be taken to keep soil moist but never wet. The seeds may not need further watering for weeks, depending on where they are kept, the natural condition of the soil, and other factors. Touch the mica preparation lightly once or twice a week and learn to feel when it is right; it should be spongily damp.

In flats or pots, sow the seeds more thinly than when planting them in the open because of a higher percentage of germination. If seedlings are too crowded they do not get off to a good start. In this case, transplant them as soon as possible so that they will have room to develop — to another flat, to small flower pots, a coldframe, or to a protected open seedbed.

Biennial and perennial seeds are started in much the same way as are those of annuals except that they are usually sown in the spring and summer preceding the year they are to bloom. The date naturally varies with conditions in different parts of the country, so consult directions on the packages.

If you do not have a greenhouse, a hotbed, or coldframe, and yet have been bitten by the bug of growing plants from seed, you can do it as suggested above by starting the seeds and later transferring them (in their flats or by transplanting) to a protected spot in the garden. In spring a temporary home might be against the south side of your house, or against a stone wall, or you might rig up a temporary coldframe from an old window sash, eliminating it when the young plants are in their permanent homes. As gardening interest grows, there is never room enough for all the interesting experiments. With the challenge of gardening in the shade, you will want to grow more and more unusual things with which most nurserymen don't want to bother.

ANNUALS AND BIENNIALS THAT BLOOM IN SHADE

Ageratum. Easily grown annual. Takes two and a half to three months for flowers to come from seeds; sow indoors accordingly. (Around March in Boston.) Fuzzy lavender heads all summer. Dwarf variety good for edging. Other varieties can be tucked in anywhere at the front of the garden.

Clarkia. Double flowers, white to pink, arranged along the stems. Grows easily where summers are not too hot. Warm, light soil. Will stand partial shade. Sow out of doors where they are to bloom.

Digitalis purpurea — Foxglove. 2–4'. Biennial that self-sows if planted in right place. Stately and distinctive. Spires of white or purple flower-thimbles give an accent to certain garden spots. Sow seeds spring or summer and carry young plants over winter in a coldframe until you know how to handle them. Need good drainage and plenty of humus in the soil to help the drainage. Water must not freeze on the crowns. Will take quite a dense shade.

Bellis perennis — English Daisy. True Daisy. A perennial treated as an annual or biennial. Low; compact; good edging plant, blooming till warm weather; blooms again when weather gets cool. Sow in summer; carry over young plants in coldframe. Set out early in spring. Likes moist, well-drained soil and will bloom for years in partial shade.

Eucharidum breweri — Fairy Fans. Closely allied to, and having the same requirements as, *Clarkia*. Leafy stem. Showy, pink flowers with honeysuckle fragrance.

Godetia grandiflora — Satin Flower. 4–12". Varieties with white, pink, red, etc., satiny-petaled flowers. Likes a cool, moist soil, sun or light shade.

Impatiens Balsamina — Garden Balsam. Shrubby little annual to 1½′. Rose-like blooms in lavender, rose, white, etc., close along the stems. Easily raised from seed. Tender, but blooms until after frost. Likes rich, sandy loam, and a little shade. Chapter 8 for other species.

Ionopsidium acaule — Diamond-Flower. 2–3′. Half-hardy perennial but treated like an annual. Profusion of tiny white or lavender flowers. Requires moist soil, partial shade. Does not like wind. Mostly grown in the West.

Lobelia. Annual Lobelias are compact little plants, excellent for edging beds. Usually blue flowers, but there is a white variety. Likes sun, but grows in partial shade.

Lobularia — Sweet Alyssum. One of most satisfactory annuals. Grows anywhere. Rounded spikes of white blossoms that bloom almost continuously through summer. In the South, it is grown (with other annuals) in winter and spring. Seeds itself everywhere. Takes some shade, particularly if it grows there of its own accord.

Lunaria — Money Plant. Honesty. 1–3′. Branching stems of bright orchid-colored flowers. Later, the covering of the seed pods can be rubbed off, leaving lovely silvery disks at ends of stems. Used for winter decorations. Let seeds fall, to grow more plants the following year.

Lychnis Coronaria — Dusty Miller. 1–2½′. Gray-green foliage interesting in the shady garden. Flowers, about 1″, on ends of many-branching stems, crimson or white. Seeds freely. Attractive young new rosettes of plants.

Matricaria — Feverfew. 1–2′. Attractive fern-like foliage. Blossoms, like daisies, or double, in profusion. Seeds itself everywhere, but is easily moved or pulled out, if not wanted. Good filler for small places, in sun or shade.

Mimulus — Monkey-Flower. Several species, some sold as varieties. 8–18″. Sow seeds in Jan. to have blooms in June, but difficult to raise from seed. Interesting spotted flowers. Like protection from wind; some shade.

Sweet William is one of the few biennials that tolerate shade.

Myosotis — Forget-Me-Not. Plant in fall for spring and summer bloom. Blue, pink, or white flowers.

Nemophila insignis — Baby-Eyes. Dwarf, compact, hairy plant. Quick-growing. Abundance of clear, blue, wide-open flowers. Low, shady ground. Native of California, but grows anywhere. Charming in rock garden.

Nicotiana affinis — Flowering Tobacco. Starry white blossoms of exquisite fragrance. Rather awkward stems to 2', should be planted near other bushier forms. Easily grown from seed and will stand partial shade. Red variety, but white is particularly lovely in the shady garden. Find new plants growing near old for replanting another year.

Nigella — Love-in-a-Mist. To 1'. Lovely lacy foliage and the bluest of blue flowers. Exquisite. Seed pods interesting. Prefers sun, but often seeds itself in shade and grows there. Does not transplant. Sow seed in fall where it is to grow.

Reseda odorata — Mignonette. Bushy annuals to 18". Should be pinched back to shape. Brownish flower spikes that have an appealing fragrance all their own. Likes lime and a moderately rich, well-drained soil. Needs shade at least part of the day.

Rudbeckia bicolor — Coneflower. Yellow, daisy-like single, or double, flowers with dark centers. Easily grown in almost any soil, sun or partial shade. Varieties in yellow, orange, mahogany. Familiar *R. hirta* (Black-Eyed Susan) tolerates partial shade too, and seeds itself.

Salpiglossis — Velvet Flower. Trumpet-shaped flowers in gorgeous velvety colors, veined with yellow, crimson, purple, etc. Plants, rather skimpy, to 18". Likes a sandy soil in half-shade. Soil not too rich gives the best colors.

Torenia — Wishbone Flower. Like miniature Snapdragons; in ivory, blue, rose. Compact, bushy plants to 1'. Floriferous. Easily grown, but used mostly in the South, where they seed by the hundreds. Good in masses in front of evergreens. Likes some shade.

Verbascum Thapsus — Common Mullein. Biennial, which seeds itself everywhere, but first year's growth is attractive gray rosette of velvety leaves. Can be transplanted or thrown away as it grows larger. Massed at the back of a border or even shrubs, its tall stateliness gives height and beauty. Tolerates some shade. *V. phoeniceum* to 5', has purple flowers, which open better if plant receives only morning and afternoon sun.

6

Bulbs Like Shade Too

✦✻✦☸✦✻✦☸✦✻✦☸✦✻✦☸✦✻✦☸✦✻✦☸✦✻✦☸✦✻✦☸✦✻✦☸✦✻✦☸✦✻✦☸✦✻✦☸

A BULB IS AN enlarged bud, a storage place for a plant's food. Fleshy scales, encasing the embryo flower, are potential leaves. These are attached in a mat at the bottom and from this the roots grow in fall and winter, drying up in early summer after the growth of the plant has stopped. *Narcissi* and Lilies are true bulbs.

There are other plants with swollen roots and stems that are often referred to as bulbs, however. Crocuses fall into this category, growing from flat, round corms 1–1½″ wide. These are solid and not scaly like true bulbs. Snowdrops and a few other members of the Amaryllis Family have bulbous roots and are referred to either as bulbous plants or bulbs. Dahlias grow from eyes in fleshy, enlarged, underground stems called tubers; while such plants as bearded Irises have an enlarged horizontal stem, called a rhizome, growing at the top of the ground. Roots come from the bottom of the rhizome and anchor the plant; from the top come the leaves and flower stems.

Hardy bulbs are those bulbs and bulbous-rooted plants which are able to live out of doors all the time. They are usually planted in the fall, when they grow roots, and their fountains of foliage are among the first of the green shoots in the spring. The flowers bloom, fade in a few weeks, and may be cut off, but the leaves of a bulb-flower should be left on and allowed to die down naturally.

The reason is that the leaves of any plant are vital in the manufacturing of a plant's food. This wonderful and intricate process involves nitrogen, phosphorus, potassium, and other chemical elements, and raw materials such as water, air, and sunlight. Soil usually contains most of the elements. Water and ample compost in the soil makes them available to the plant, so that the tiny root hairs can absorb them, and they will be carried upward to the leaves and stems. While this is happening the plant's leaves take in oxygen and carbon dioxide from the air; and, with energy derived from the sun, proceed with the business of food manufacturing, called *photosynthesis.*

This process goes on during spring and early summer until the leaves die down. Underground, the bulb waxes fat and pregnant with the life within it. It is an entirely new plant, which if it has been properly nurtured, is complete with leaves and flower bud. Often it can sustain itself without benefit of soil until the plant blooms again. Thus, we have the phenomena of Paper-white Narcissi, Hyacinths, and other bulbs blooming in water only. Consequently, to cut off leaves of any bulb-flower before they have completed their job, not only seriously impairs the efficiency of the bulb, but is apt to deplete it altogether.

The wonderful thing about many of the hardy bulbs is that they can be planted in the shade, or at least in partial shade. Though their leaves need the sun, they receive enough in winter and early spring before the overhanging branches shut it out.

As a matter of fact, most of the blub flowers thrive better under trees where there is plenty of light and air than in a hot dry area. In light woodlands they are protected from burning wind and sun, that dry foliage too quickly. In woods, or under trees where there is a natural mulch of wood debris, the dying foliage is not noticed. And there is no more welcome sight in April, before the trees have donned their summer green, than to look across the sun-spattered under-growth and see cheery colonies of Daffodils and clumps of white Narcissi.

If you have no woodland but are blessed with trees, plant your bulb flowers at their feet — a shaggy Pine with a few buttercup-flowers of *Adonis amurensis* in the garden beneath. Or make the single Oak at the end of your garden, a prelude to spring, with clumps of golden Daffodils leading to it. Just picture the frilled orange cups of some of the Jonquils near the lively gray of a Yellow-Wood Tree, or a White Ash look-ing down on the speckled bells of *Fritillaria meleagris*. On the other hand, *F. imperialis* calls for the majestic arms of an Elm or an old Chinese Scholar-Tree (*Sophora japonica*) to honor its scarlet "crown imperial"! Trees like Maples and Beeches that crowd numerous roots close to the top of the soil should have their bulbs near the outside edges of their shadows to escape as many roots as possible.

In modern gardens, scaled to small houses and yards, the smaller trees are used for shade and woodsy effects. Little bulb flowers make themselves at home beneath them. There

are white *Chionodoxa* to blend with the pinky purple of
Magnolia, late-blooming *Scilla hispanica* to deepen the blush
of a pale flowering Crab Apple. The pure white Star Magnolia *(M. stellata)* is set off by the vivid red of early-flowering
Tulipa eichleri.

Craggy native Witch-Hazel, not appreciated nearly
enough in modern gardens, likes yellow *Narcissus poetaz* or
the early blooms of Winter Aconite. Artistic tiers of Dogwood
are seen when Snowdrops lift white heads beneath their
boughs. And suddenly, with Snowdrops here, anticipation
sharpens to see those tree buds starting into leaf. Hopes rise;
Spicebush outlines itself in yellow in the woods, and Shadblow unfolds in clouds of white. Bumps of green stud the
earth beneath. The raking of last fall's litter uncovers Narcissi
leaves in green fountains. The buds grow fat and finally
unfold into golden trumpets of brilliant orange cups frilled
with white petals.

Perhaps you like your hardy bulbs in front of your evergreen foundation group, a clump of early Snowdrops near
the house within the protecting arms of *Chamaecyparis,* or
a row of Crocuses under the *Taxus,* or a colony of species
Narcissi in a small intimate area where their delicate beauty
will not be lost in the review of larger blossoms. This is ideal
for those fastidious people who like bulb flowers but not the
unsightliness of their dying foliage. The foliage is not noticed
among evergreen shrubs. The blossoms brighten the scene of
early spring, are gone before the beds must be edged, the
lawn trimmed, and fading ribbon-leaves can be tucked down
at the foot of the shrub branches caught by the sun's eye but
not by man's. Or, when the foliage is quite limp, lay it on
the ground and lose it in a light peat-moss mulch, which
gives a natural tidiness to your beds. For the lazy gardener,

bulbs among the shrubs is a two-in-one bed proposition. It's more sensible than it sounds, for who wants to edge both a shrub-border and a bed of bulbs when it can be combined into one activity and probably be more picturesque besides?

If you're fond of your garden and expand your cultivating activities to include a perennial border, you'll want a few bulbs there. How pretty they look on the flat earth with the green of later flowers just beginning to grow. If foliage becomes unsightly in the neatness of other green growth, turn it back upon the earth and hold it down with a small rock, and let other perennials hide it as they grow up around it.

In general, the time to plant spring bulbs is in the fall. Get good ones from a reputable firm. Cheap bulbs may give satisfaction, but the success of your bulbs depends a great deal on the treatment they have had before coming into your hands. Hardy bulbs take several years of growing to reach blooming size. Each year the leaves must be allowed to come up, make nourishment for the bulb, and die down naturally. Often you can buy small blooming-size bulbs. In fact, a concern that specializes in bulbs usually offers bulbs of various sizes — small, large, and jumbo.

Most people now leave their hardy bulbs in the ground throughout the year. Time was when they were planted in great beds, particularly showy Tulips, then lifted and replaced with annuals. But the tendency in these days of scarce garden labor, is to semi-naturalize Tulips, as well as other bulb flowers, to grow clumps of 6-12 in the perennial border or in some other cultivated place, and leave them there year after year. Subsequent bloomings are usually not so perfect as that of the first year, but new little bulblets keep sending up leaves and finally bloom. If planted in quantities for dramatic effect, a number of the same color should be used together. Mixed colors in a mass do not contribute to good garden design.

Tulips do not adapt themselves as readily to naturalizing as Narcissi and some of the smaller bulbs. Neither will they take as much shade.

Tulips like good drainage and deep, rich soil full of rotted manure, compost, and bone meal. Keep enriching the soil yearly around them, give them as much sun as possible, let them continue to grow in a clump, and divide only when the leaves seem too numerous to stay in the same location.

Narcissi, Scilla, and other bulbs prefer the same home year after year. They do not have to be dug up except when they have grown into large, tight clusters crying for breathing space. You'll suspect something of the kind because blossoms will be fewer and smaller, the buds will blast, and the foliage have a tired look. Then, as the leaves are dying down, dig up the whole clump. You'll find as many as sixty or seventy, even one hundred in a compact ball of bulbs. Replanted, some of the smaller ones may not bloom the following year because they need time to grow to blooming size, but place them where you won't have to worry about them, and in a year or two you'll have quantities of blossoms.

Established in woods or fields, and allowed to fend for themselves instead of being coddled with extra cultivation and fertilizer, hardy bulbs don't multiply readily. But in time, they too will have to be divided and replenished. People speak of Narcissi as having "run out," when they find them in a tangle of grass and other growth. It's merely that they're starved or suffocated, and need more room.

Directions for planting usually come with bulbs bought from a reliable seed-house. Like most plants bulbs need good drainage, and a sandy loam is best. However, if yours is a clayey soil dig the hole deep and mix several trowels of sand at the bottom before setting in the bulb.

If the soil is poor and hard, put it into condition a few weeks beforehand. Dig deeper than planting depth; if you add manure or any fertilizer to the soil, mix it *well* into the soil. Do not allow it to come into contact with the bulb or it will burn and probably destroy it. Compost from the compost pile is much safer to use and bulb-flowers love it.

Most bulbs are planted at a depth about four times their height. Plant them as soon as they arrive. Narcissi like to start putting out roots as early as September. If they are planted too late, the proper root growth is not attained, and the flowers don't blossom to their best ability.

Grape Hyacinths like to be planted early and send up leaves in late summer. Tulips can be planted any time until the ground freezes, as their best root growth comes in the cold weather. Like other plants, each type of bulb has its own characteristics. The wonder is that given similar garden conditions, and more or less the same treatment, so many of them do so well. They are easy to grow!

In planning the pictures to be made by your bulb flowers, consider the size of the garden and yard, distances and places from which they are to be viewed, and other nearby plants blooming at the same time. Small bulbs are best placed near the house, alongside a path, under small shrubs, at the front of a group of perennials, or in some other spot that is likely to be seen without difficulty. Many times a mass of them can be used under deciduous trees with a ground-cover such as Pachysandra or Periwinkle to take over after the flowers have disappeared.

To give any show, the small bulbs should be planted in groups of nine to fifteen, or more, if they are to be viewed from a distance. In small clumps, set them 3 inches apart; in larger clumps, particularly if they are to be allowed to naturalize, set them 4 inches apart and forget them.

Small species Tulips and Narcissi are treated more as rock-garden subjects, or planted in places where their delicate beauty can be appreciated. Larger Tulips like at least 6 inches to themselves, while Narcissi enjoy 8 inches and more so they have room to spread.

If you've never grown lilies, you have a treat in store for you. They are beautiful and charming flowers, many of them of such stately grace that we marvel they grow so easily for amateur gardeners.

Of exquisite perfection and purity, some varieties seem to belong only to elegant, formal gardens, yet they are at home anywhere. A modest garden they grace with natural charm, like royalty in a cottage. They raise a mediocre garden to outstanding artistry by adding a touch of distinction. Other varieties are flamboyant and gay, generous with reds and yellows, but never cheapening their surroundings. A few have been kept in their original wild state, belonging to shaded woodlands and wild flower retreats. All are beautiful, with so much individual appeal that it is difficult to choose among them. Many have a delightful fragrance. Best of all, perhaps, is the fact that they blossom in summer, when the great splash of spring bloom is only a memory.

Lilies are distinctive in many ways. Each has its own set of characteristics. The white varieties (*L. regale, L. candidum,* etc.) are as different from the yellow and orange types (*L. philadelphicum* and *L. tigrinum*) as they can be. Blos-

Lilies and tuberous Begonias against a Yew hedge, with a fountain as a focal point.

soms with recurve petals (*L. Speciosum*) do not seem at all like the deep funnels of the *Centifolium* hybrids. Most of them grow best in an acid soil, yet a few must have lime. All should be planted in late summer or fall, immediately upon arrival from the nursery. Unlike spring-flowering bulbs, Lilies should not be allowed to dry out.

Whereas the hardy spring bulbs are planted approximately four times their height, Lilies in general should be planted two or three times as deep as they are long. This varies with the type of Lily; there are two classes — those that grow roots only from the bottom of the bulb, and those that grow roots along the stem up to ground level, as well as from the bottom. The latter types are planted deeper, to insure as much root growth as possible.

Because Lilies are so different, the potential Lily-grower must rely on a catalogue to tell him what, how, and where to plant, until he has learned something about the Family. All Lilies can be grown in some parts of the country, but only a few can be raised in all parts of the country. This is due partly to soil conditions, and partly to the type of winter in the particular area.

In some parts of the country, Lilies object to the heaving of the ground, due to continual freezing and thawing. They do not like to be frozen in heavy wet soil in winter, or to lie in a puddle in spring. In other words, good drainage is essential. Plenty of leafmold, rough compost, and well-rotted manure enrich the soil, as well as conditioning it to alleviate winter freezing. A mulch helps to keep the roots cool, and holds the moisture during hot dry weather.

Besides the better known hardy bulbs which are planted in the fall are a few lesser bulbs that are fun to try. The easily blooming fall Crocus and allied plants give you delightful surprises by simply appearing! *Montbretia* offers another kind of surprise by growing only foliage for several years after you have planted and forgotten it; then suddenly starting to bloom.

Tuberous Begonias, although not hardy, must be included here. They are a *must* for shady places, with their lovely, lush blossoms of exquisite colors. And they prefer the shade — not a dense, smothering shade, but an airy sun-filtered shade. This does not mean that they do not like sun. Theoretically they bloom better if exposed to early morning sun and spattered sunlight, but they also bloom in an unbelievable amount of shade.

Lifting them from the ground and carrying them over the winter may seem like too big a price to pay for a little summer bloom. Like most garden duties, it's simple, once you have the habit.

Dig them as soon as the frost comes, else their leaves melt away and you can't find them. Let them dry a few days in the sun and rub off excess dirt. Store in peat moss in a cool (45–50°) dark cellar that is not too dry, or plant in bulb pan, or in individual pots in rough humus. Water them about twice during the winter, just enough to keep them from drying out. At the end of March or April, bring them into the open, give one good watering and wait for small nublets of new growth to appear. Water if very dry, but don't do much watering until the first leaves look like leaves. Begonias do not like to be wet, but they do like moisture in both soil and atmosphere. Rough humus and peat moss keeps soil in good condition.

Begonias will survive poor cellar conditions, but they grow a little spindling if there is too little light. Plant them outdoors when their second leaves are established and after the ground has become warm (May–June). Plant them directly in the earth, or in pots set into the ground out of the way of dogs and children. See that they have plenty of rough compost, light and air, and stake if necessary. In July they start blooming.

(*Gottscho-Schleisner*)

Scilla hispanica grows in quite dense shade.

Bulbs That Like, or Will Tolerate, Some Shade
Fall-Planting

Anemone coronaria — Poppy Anemone. Not quite hardy in the North. Worth trying in a sheltered spot. Beautiful. Exquisite colors. Keep bulb dry before planting.

Asphodeline lutea — King's Spear. 2–4′. Grayish, leafy flower stems. Racemes of fragrant yellow flowers 6–18″. Plenty of humus. Light shade.

Camassia. To 15″. Grass-like foliage. Blue stars or white in graceful raceme. Recommended for shade, but it should be a light shade, or where sun falls four to five hours a day. Good drainage.

Chionodoxa — Glory-of-The-Snow. Beautiful blue reflexed petals with white stripe, turned to the sky. Naturalize easily under deciduous trees or where they receive light in spring (until foliage dies down). White and pink varieties.

Crocus. Also likes sun in spring. Good under tall trees or at edge of woodland where lawn doesn't have to be mowed until late. Moth balls keep rabbits away from tender buds. *Fall Crocus.* Bulbs planted July-August. Similar to spring crocus, with no leaves. Leaves come up in spring, like grass. Don't pull them up.

Cyclamen neapolitanum. Dainty miniature Cyclamen of rosy pink in fall. Planted in August, however. Must have right conditions; plenty of humus, but rather dry, with lime added. Nothing is sweeter when this is a success. Rock garden.

Eranthus hyemalis — Winter Aconite. Cheery, yellow blossome resembling *Adonis amurensis.* (Both of Buttercup Family.) Early. Green sepals, like collar, set off the flowers. Hardy. Easy to grow, persisting for years in a neglected spot.

Fritillaria imperialis — Crown Imperial. 3–4′. Large clusters of yellow or crimson flowers at top of stem. Interesting. Not

(Gottscho-Schleisner)

Clumps of cheery Daffodils brighten up rocks.

reliably hardy north of New York, but they have been grown in New England. Plant 6–8″ deep, protected shady spot, good drainage. *F. meleagris* — Guinea-hen Flower. Hardier. Hanging checkered bells. Lower-growing. Good in rock garden. Partial or light shade. Several varieties, some native to West.

Galanthus — Snowdrop. One of earliest and most appealing of all bulb flowers. Clumps of ribbon-like foliage with nod-

(*Paul E. Genereux*)

Fritillaria meleagris growing in the shade of a White Ash.

ding, dainty white flowers. To 10″. Plant near house, or where you can appreciate their early bloom. Hardy, likes good drainage and humus. A warm spot brings flowers earlier.

Leucojum — Snowflake. Gracefully drooping white bell-like flowers. Interesting green-tipped petals. Does best in shady garden. Plant well, with humus, and do not disturb for years. Good for cutting.

Lilium — Lily. Beautiful and charming. Easy to grow. Bulbs are planted in summer or fall, or whenever the nursery sends them, immediately upon arrival. Because Lilies are all so different, the potential lily-grower must rely on catalogues to tell what, how, and where to plant. On the Pacific Coast with mild winter climate and high humidity, practically all the Lilies can be grown. Interesting hybrids have been originated there; the Bellingham Hybrids (orange-yellow, etc.). Next favored spot is New England. In other parts of the country, fewer varieties can be grown.

Good drainage is absolutely essential to all Lilies. Most of them like an acid soil, but a few must have lime. Some need sun; others want light shade. Most like cool feet, a rich, sandy loam with old manure and compost dug in. A light mulch of either dug around bulbs in the fall helps alleviate freezing and thawing, which Lilies do not like.

Lilies must be planted immediately upon arrival. Unlike other bulbs, they do not like to be dried out. There is almost a continual growing process; do not remove roots that might come on a bulb. Some lilies grow roots only at the bottom of the bulb; others have stem roots also. The more roots any plant has, the better flowering there will be.

Lilium Hansonii, L. Henryi, and hybrids. — Excellent Oriental types. Robust. Strong-growing. Prefer partial shade so that blossoms won't bleach. Yellow to orange and allied colors. To 8′.

L. Martagon — Turks-Cap Lily. Purplish or white drooping flowers with recurved petals in tiers. To 6′. Sun or shade.

L. philadelphicum — Wood Lily (East). Yellow to scarlet. Dry, acid soil, preferably at the edges of woodlands. *L. umbellatum* (West) and hybrids are hardy and similar to preceding.

L. regale — Regal Lily. 3–4′. Large, white, trumpet-shaped. Delightful fragrance.

L. tigrinum — Tiger Lily. 3–4′. Reflexed petals. Burnt orange. Hardy. Shade.

Mertensia virginica — Virginia Blue Bells. 1–2′. Grows quickly. Hanging pink and blue bells. Dainty and attractive. Easy. Place behind foliage plant, as leaves die down after blooming period.

Muscari — Grape-Hyacinth. Like blue bunch of grapes at the top of stem, 7–10″. Sun or shade. Plant immediately on receiving, so leaf growth can start. Small bulbs; good in large drifts. Divide when crowded. Variety, *plumosum,* violet colored, unusual, different.

Narcissus — Daffodil, Jonquil, Narcissus. To some people the terms are interchangeable. They are all *Narcissus.* Many beautiful and practical varieties have been hybridized from the species. Mostly yellows and whites, with new introductions of pink varieties. Those with large "trumpets" are usually called Daffodils, in both yellow and white; also bicolor. Jonquils are usually known as the yellow flowers clustered on one stem. Fragrant. Narcissi are usually late and single, or the large, single flowers with smallish or medium-sized cups in either the same, or a different color from the perianth. They are all delightful and easily grown. Under trees or in sun-spattered woodlands, they naturalize beautifully as well as in open fields. Under cultivation, in better soil, and with more room, they grow faster and have to be separated every four to five years, when clump grows tight and buds blast. Dig them up as foliage dies down, separate, and replant immediately. Never cut foliage. Choose large Narcissi to be seen at a distance; the smaller ones for close-at-hand, intimate gardens. Miniature species are excellent for rock gardens and other small areas.

Ornithogalum umbellatum — Star-of-Bethlehem. White, starry flowers among heavy grass-like foliage. Takes quite a dense shade. Hardy to Boston.

Puschkinia — Lebanon Squill. Bells along stem, like small Hyacinth. Grayish blue. Interesting for rock garden or small area.

Scilla. Charming small bulb flower. Blue and white. Treatment same as *Chionodoxa.* Drainage. Grows everywhere if not watched. Delightful. *S. hispanica S. Campanulata* — Wood Hyacinth. Blooms with the Tulips. Grows in quite a dense shade, and thrives under firs and hemlocks. Pink, blue, white. Separate only when clumps get too large.

Tulipa. Tulip. Probably most popular of all bulb flowers. Stem to 2', with several long pointed leaves, and topped with a bright colored single (usually) blossom. Colors exquisite. Petals of satiny texture. Lovely; easy to grow. Likes a deep rich soil with good drainage. Does not naturalize well in woodlands but will stand some shade with good soil. Number of interesting Species Tulips: *T. clusiana* — dainty cherry-rose and white striped. Does well in South and North; *T. Eichleri,* with pointed red petals; and others, very early. Different types have been developed from various species Tulips; Early Single and Double, Triumph, Breeder, Cottage, Darwin, etc. Mostly chosen by variety name. Bulbs need not be lifted. Small bulblets develop around them and finally bloom, while old bulb dies out.

SUMMER BULBS THAT TOLERATE SOME SHADE
Spring-planting

Begonia, Tuberous. Lush foliage. Spectacular, cleanly-beautiful flowers in yellow, white, orange, red, pink, salmon. Double, frilled, picotee, and other fancy varieties — all beautiful. Like rough, humusy soil with good drainage. Easy to start in house in 7" pots, or seedbox, in March (North). Keep damp, not wet. Plant under trees when ground is warm. When frost strikes, dig up immediately.

Colchicum — Meadow Saffron. Flowers similar to spring and fall Crocus. Rise without leaves, and unexpectedly in August to September. Cabbage-like leaves in spring die in early summer.

Montbretia (Tritonia). Thin, sword-like leaves. Spikes of smallish, funnel-shaped flowers toward end of summer. Yellows predominate. Interesting manner of growing. Sun or partial shade. Rich soil. Hardy to New York, but grown out-of-doors in New England. Good drainage.

PART TWO

Foliage and Woody Plants

7

Ferns in the Shady Garden

✣✿✣✿✣✿✣✿✣✿✣✿✣✿✣✿✣✿✣✿✣✿✣✿✣✿✣✿✣✿✣✿

FERNS HAVE A distinct personality from the moment the first "fiddle heads" start to uncurl from the harsh spring earth, to the completion of their growth in the fall. What can be lovelier than the stately reddish brown croziers of the large *Osmunda* ferns rising beside a gray rock, or behind yellow primroses? What more appealing, than a tiny *Woodsia* or *Woodfern*, growing from a rock crevice where by chance a spore fell? Finding little new ferns under an apple tree or in the wild garden, delights the plant-lover who introduces ferns to his garden.

Ferns are ideal subjects in dense, or partial shade, for with the exception of one or two varieties, they prefer shade to sun. Some thrive in both, but most like a moist location, though many will endure remarkably dry conditions. All of them like compost and leafmold.

Their garden uses are many. Planted among spring perennials whose foliage dies after bloom, ferns make excellent covers. When narcissi blossoms no longer dance, fern foliage

Ferns actually prefer shade to sun.

can hide the browning ribbon-leaves. Plant them in unused places that you dress up in the spring with daffodils, and let them grow freely there. In smaller or more select gardens, use ferns with distinctive foliage, growing from a root-crown — the Christmas Fern with its crisp, evergreen look and Purple Cliff Brake with a blue-gray color and unusual frond forms.

Ferns are excellent for the north side of a house. Let the long plumes of Goldie's Fern, Ostrich, or another large species break the monotoy of a cement foundation. If your shrubs grow spindling, plant some of the lower-growing ferns — the woodferns, Christmas Fern, or a clump of Maidenhair Fern, to "dress up" the lower branches of the shrubs.

Against a low stone wall and as companions to rocks in the rock garden, ferns are colorful and graceful. They love rocks and old stumps. If given a chance the Christmas Fern and Polypody will blanket whole tops of large boulders and logs as they do in the woods.

Ferns add a touch of the wild to the most modest collection of wild flowers. If a breath of woodland is desired with one or two oaks and evergreens, ferns help create the illusion. They are invaluable on banks of a brook, or at the edge of a pool, particularly an informal pool amid rocks. To a formal garden they add elegance and grace, and take attention from the poor or uninteresting foliage of other perennials. Birds love them, often stealing the white cottony substance from the uncurled fronds for the lining of their nests.

With the exception of one or two varieties, which require special conditions, ferns are easy to grow. Though many ferns will survive under unsatisfactory conditions the best way to grow healthy plants is to try to duplicate the conditions under which they are found growing naturally. If you are transplanting them from the wild, look around and see what kinds of trees grow near them. If oaks and evergreens, you can assume there is acid soil beneath. But if there are beeches or limestone cliffs nearby, an alkaline or neutral soil is indicated. Ferns such as Purple Cliff Brake, Rock Brake, Walking

Many ferns will endure remarkably dry conditions.
Hay scented fern and starry chickweed.

Fern, Maidenhair Fern, found near limestone, should have limestone in order to thrive — a condition easy to duplicate in a garden merely by adding ground limestone. Most ferns, however, are indifferent to soil pH as long as they have plenty of leafmold and compost.

Romantic legends have been built around ferns. Among Germanic and Celtic nations they were considered sacred and auspicious, with the power of bringing good luck to certain people. In medieval days the "seed" of the fern was supposed to impart to the owner the ability to resist magical powers and incantations. Our ancestors thought fern seed invisible; hence, he who could wear fern-seed about his person could become invisible also.

Shakespeare recognized this belief of years ago, for he makes Gadshill say in *Henry IV*, "We steal in the castle, cocksure; we have the receipt of fern-seed, we walk invisible."

But in spite of the fact that the ancients thought there must be fern seeds, ferns have never borne flowers. They were supposed to have done so in the days before the birth of Jesus. On the Eve of the Nativity, when all other plants burst into bloom, the fern alone, did not. Hence it was condemned forever afterward to go flowerless.

Ancient botanists were mystified by the odd non-flowering plants. They studied small ferns apparently growing near their parents. How did they reproduce themselves if there were no seeds? The manner of this mysterious process was not discovered until 1848. Even now, although many people recognize the little dark dots on the under side of fern fronds as *spore-cases* that have something to do with the development of new plants, they actually do not know how this is brought about.

Spores are not like seeds, though it is true that they are

contained in cases that burst open when the spores are ripe. Those falling on favorable soil conditions, germinate and produce what is called a *prothallium*. On the under side of the *prothallium* grow fine root-like hairs and two sets of organs corresponding to the pistils and stamens of a flower. Fertilization follows, along with the birth of the new little fern. But it takes seven years for that fern to mature. In the meantime, the young ferns often fool even experts into thinking they are ferns of a different variety.

There are about 6000 species of ferns in the world. Most of these grow in the tropics and constitute but a few of the numbers that inhabited the earth millions of years ago. Some of these ancient ferns achieved enormous sizes and are with us today in the form of coal.

To a gardener who has never experimented with ferns, one variety might be very like another. It is only when he starts examining their fronds, lacy or leathery, plumed or triangular, that he finds the great variety of form and substance in this highest form of non-flowering plants.

As of old, the fern foliage consists of fronds. Most of these are cut entirely or part way to the midvein. If cut all the way, so each segment seems like a frond in its own right, the front is referred to as being once-pinnate, and each segment is called a *pinna*. When the *pinnae* are, in turn, cut again into segments, the frond is twice-pinnate and the segments of the pinnae called *pinnules*.

In most ferns the fertile fronds look very much like other fronds but have their spore-cases on the backs, each variety having its own time of ripening, anywhere from late June through September. In some cases the fertile fronds have an individuality all their own. Those on the Interrupted Fern are taller than the sterile fronds, with several pairs of the middle or fruiting *pinnae,* brownish and dried-up looking, so the *pinnae* of these fronds indeed, look "interrupted."

Like most plants, ferns are best moved while dormant; in early spring before they have begun their season's growth, or in late summer or fall after growth has stopped. Large ferns are difficult to move, particularly when found growing in swamp conditions with numerous other plants. Their roots are bulky and entwined with roots. Ferns such as the Cinnamon Fern grow as individuals but from root-stocks attached to others in the vicinity, so they are difficult to separate. The Interrupted Fern is not so deeply planted, but is hard to move from the wild except when small. It is easier to dig up mature plants of the smaller type ferns and those which send up individual fronds along creeping roots. Such are the Common Polypody, with roots close to the top of the soil, the Hay-Scented Fern, and the Massachusetts Fern.

Ferns with fronds rising from a crown like the Christmas Fern, and Woodferns, make better garden subjects than those which send up fronds continuously along the rootstock. These latter (Hay-Scented Fern, Lady Fern, Massachusetts Fern, etc.) are better for naturalizing in odd shady corners where almost nothing else will grow, or for serving as ground-cover, or background for some of the wild flowers. They love a little attention, however, and are apt to take over when given good soil conditions; the difficulty becomes one of restricting them rather than encouraging them to grow.

When moving ferns from the wild, try to set them exactly as they were in their natural homes. In the case of most ferns, the crowns should not be completely buried. If this does not look well in your garden scheme, mulch with peat moss or other attractive mulching material lightly around the crown. It is well to keep ferns mulched anyway; in winter, to protect the crowns and roots and keep the soil from too much freezing and thawing, and in summer to keep the roots cool and moist.

A word should be said about the confusion of fern names. Whereas other plants can usually be specifically identified by their scientific names, ferns are most competently known by their common names, because of disagreement over their scientific nomenclature. Consider the Beech Fern, of which there are two varieties. What I think of as the Winged Beech Fern, is listed botanically in one source as *Thelypteris hexagonoptera* and in another as *Phegopteris hexagonoptera*. A third authority calls it *Dryopteris hexagonoptera*. All seem to agree on the term *hexagonoptera* which means six-angled and winged. The winged is apt, for the lower *pinnae* (larger and broader than the others) grow out at an angle to the main stem and are rather reminiscent of wings.

The Woodferns are even more confusing since there is a greater number of them. They hybridize shamefully, so that you no sooner have one set of characteristics ascribed to a particular variety than it turns out to be something else. But don't let it throw you! Even the experts don't agree on the scientific names, though everyone seems to be able to talk the common language.

Below are listed a few of the more common ferns that the gardener might like to include in a wild garden, along the banks of a stream, in woodsy patches, or even in a perennial border. You don't have to learn their names in order to enjoy them, as long as you choose the ones that will grow easily. Dig in plenty of leafmold and humus when you plant them.

Well-Known Ferns for the Shady Garden

Berry Bladder Fern — *Crystopteris bulbifera*. 1–3′. Bi-pinnate; crowded with toothed pinnules. Little bulblets from the underside of the mature fronds in midsummer, root quickly when they fall onto moist soil. Tolerant of acid conditions, but prefer limestone.

Bracken — *Pteridium latiusculum.* 2–3′. Apt to spring up unbidden in your garden. Broad, triangular fronds; three distinct sections.

Christmas Fern — *Polystichum acrostichoides.* 1–2′. An excellent garden subject, especially for rock gardens. Evergreen fronds, rather leathery, once-pinnate, with the *pinnae* edged with tiny bristling teeth.

Cinnamon Fern — *Osmunda cinnamonea.* 3–5′. Vigorous grower. Graceful, attractive background ferns. Fertile fronds early, in form of little croziers; green, turning brown. Tangled black roots. Prefers moist shade.

Common Polypody — *Polypodium virginianum.* 10–12″. Evergreen. Confused with the Christmas Fern, but not so attractive. Grows easily; withstands some dryness. Blankets boulders and fallen logs in the woods. Equally at home in the cultivated garden. Southern species is the Resurrection Fern, *Polypodium polypodioides.*

Common Woodfern — *Thelypteris intermedia.* To 2′. Lovely, lacy, bi-pinnate, often tri-pinnate. Root crown above surface of the ground. Beautiful garden specimen; evergreen. Other woodferns are often similar.

Crested Woodfern — *Thelypteris cristata.* 12–24″. Listed in nurseries, as *Dryopteris cristata.* Foliage, lacy and evergreen; fronds narrower and shorter than those of preceding species. Grows in shaded swamps; likes moisture and humus.

Goldies Fern — *Thelypteris goldiana.* To 5′. Wide stately fronds of unparalleled beauty. Easily established.

Interrupted Fern — *Osmunda claytoniana.* To 3′. Similar to preceding and to Cinnamon Fern. Fertile fronds; interrupted. Fuzzy growth around fronds in spring of this and other *Os-*

mundas, is what birds steal for their nests. Crown of root-stock should not be covered when transplanting.

Maidenhair Fern — *Adiantum pedatum.* Lovely, lacy. Graceful fronds seem to grow in a circular form, unfolding from delicate croziers of a soft pinky brown tone. Rich moist humus on the alkaline side.

New York Fern — *Thelypteris noveboracensis.* To 18″. Average garden soil. Bright green plumy fronds. Lower *pinnae* shorter toward the bottom. Grows well any shady place, but will take over if not watched. Withstands drought.

Ostrict Fern — *Pteritis nodulosa.* To 6′. Tall, graceful fronds, reminiscent of ostrich plumes. Fertile fronds; short and stiff. Tips of the young sterile fronds used as "fiddle-heads greens."

Purple Cliff-Brake — *Pellaea atropurpurea.* 12–24″. Interesting. Different. Fronds, once-pinnate near top; bi-pinnate below. Bluish green. Sun or shade. Grows near limestone.

Royal Fern — *Osmunda regalis.* 4–5′. Graceful and lovely. Young fronds uncurl in a coppery pink color. Spore-cases of fertile fronds like richly-colored brownish flowers. Moisture. Humus.

Sensitive Fern — *Onoclea sensibilis.* To 15″. Not as pretty nor graceful as other ferns. Easily identified; the fertile frond topped with berry-like spore-cases.

Walking Fern — *Camptosorus rhizophyllus.* Distinctive and unusual. Hard to establish. Long, simple fronds, like narrow heart with long tip, from which little new ferns grow. Has been known to grow in acid soil and among limestone ledges, in dry, rocky places and in moist woodland.

Winged Beechfern — *Thelypteris hexagonoptera.* The triangular-shaped fronds, with lower *pinnae* much longer than the others. The color is fresh green all summer, but fronds wither with frost.

8

Other Foliage Plants and House Plants

✧✳✦☉✧✳✦☉✧✳✦☉✧✳✦☉✧✳✦☉✧✳✦☉✧✳✦☉✧✳✦☉✧✳✦☉✧✳✦☉✧✳✦☉✧✳✦☉✧✳✦☉

PLANTS VALUED CHIEFLY for their foliage are of importance to the shady garden. With fewer flowers we have to rely on leaves of distinctive shades and on variegated foliage. There is variety in their forms and outlines, in their textures, and very feel, as well as in the shapes of individual plants. Consider these factors when planning a shady garden, for the judicious grouping of the right plants together can make all the difference in the world to your garden pictures.

When we do not expect riotous color (mostly in the form of annuals) our awareness is sharpened to the possibilities of leaves and of what the foliage of one plant does to, and with, that of another. An extreme example would be the red Norway maple (*Acer platanoides schwedleri*) and the red Japanese maple (*A. palmatum atropurpureum*) placed side by side. To the casual observer they would be merely two red maples, each lost in the other's beauty. But set either tree near something green and immediately it commands attention.

Contrast in shapes and heights contributes to the creation of garden-pictures in both sunny and shady gardens, but it is even more important in the latter. Three upright yews marching to nowhere don't mean anything; but choose them of varying heights, set them in a triangular formation with the apex toward the back, and you have a picture. Plant an upright columnar evergreen and build it down with a spreading evergreen in front of and a little to either side, and you have a simple planting that is good to look at, whether for a landscaping effect near the house or in an area where it can become the background for a flowering shrub or tree.

Shapes and textures of leaves, when well combined, make a vast difference in the beauty of a garden. A needled evergreen next to a broad-leaved evergreen gives greater significance to a planting than two needled evergreens set side by side — unless they are planted that way for a purpose. A spray of Pfitzer Juniper reaching out over the end of a laurel branch calls forth exclamations of appreciation.

Thuja and *Chamaecyparis* greatly enhance the Japanese *Andromeda,* with very shiny evergreen leaves. Because their colors are so similar, a *Taxus* planted next to a Rhododendron might be lost, were it not for the contrast in shape and texture of their foliage. In large plantings a Rhododendron makes an arresting focal point against the low branches of white pines. Similarly, an umbrella pine *(Sciadopitys verticillata),* with its unique shape and whorls of coarse, needle-like foliage, can serve as a focal point against a large mass of Rhododendrons.

Smaller-foliaged plants contribute their share to the overall plan. Little garden areas within larger garden areas! A low-growing evergreen such as *Pieris floribunda* becomes the background for a plant snuggling close at its feet. Small Boxwood can be held down by *Viola odoratum* — a bed of perfumed delight in early spring, with foliage never too coarse or rank for the delicate leaves of the Box. The bold, divided foliage of the Christmas-Rose and Lenten-Rose are a good contrast for a bed of *Vinca,* with small glossy leaves to protect the *Helleborus* while decorating its stark stems.

In this chapter we include house plants; first, because many of them are foliage plants, and second, a number of them, with their ability to withstand lack of sun in our homes, grow well in the shade. If rightly used they can give many a necessary lift to a difficult shady spot. Too many people simply "dump" house plants under a tree and forget them for the summer, but they can work both winter and summer. Make use of them, display them. Plant them where they'll add to — not detract from your garden-pictures.

Sansevieria is greatly maligned; it gets kicked around and neglected. "The Night Club Plant" someone once called it, because it is seen in dim corners of dingy night clubs. Its snaky leaves usually don't look dead until they are. Yet *Sansevieria* is an attractive plant when well-used and placed to good advantage. In the far South it grows in tall colonies, dressing up the lower portions of tree trunks. It can do the same in the North, if taken indoors before frost strikes. Let one plant serve as an accent in a small garden area. Left in the pot, or taken out, place it where it can be the tallest of a group, and build up to it so that it will serve as the focal point of a small garden-picture. In the fall repot it with new earth and let it be the dominant silhouette of your indoor garden.

Once in a while, even in shaded gardens there are small beds that one likes to turn over to something besides a permanent ground-cover. For this purpose the second of our common house plants — the *Semperflorens* type of Begonia — can be used to fill a need rather than be cast aside for the summer months.

Begonias are easy to root, in water or earth. Start taking cuttings in March and set them out in the garden when danger of frost is over. You can do this even though the roots have only been grown in water. Treat them as any annual, pressing the earth gently about the roots and keeping the plants covered for a few days if the weather is sunny or windy. Begonias treated this way are a joy, and are good for fill-ins in places that receive different amounts of sunlight through the day. They'll grow in the sun with "sunburnt" foliage but prolific bloom; they'll grow in light shade with large and lovely flowers; in deeper shade, with lush foliage and fewer flowers, and they'll even exist in very dense shade. If they grow spindling, pinch them back and tuck the pinched off slips into the ground in a barren spot and they, too, will grow. For winter plants make cuttings in late summer and take them in before frost comes.

Coleus is another house plant that has been in disfavor of late years, perhaps because it is so easy to grow. Sometimes it is the difficult plants — like problem children — that inspire the most love and interest. Coleus has no appealing blossom like that of Arbutus and Pansies, but it has beautiful leaves, colorful enough to vie with any bright bloom.

Being another "easy rooter," small plants can be grown for various odd spots in the shady garden. Cities and parks include them in designs made with other bedding plants. We can use them in our more simple garden layouts. If you need a touch of something bright to contrast with the green on either side of that little garden bench, try a good-sized Coleus. If you would like to inspire the summer appearance of *Vinca* or violet leaves, try a grouping of brilliant Coleus foliage as a focal point.

As shrubs planted around or near a house are supposed to enhance the building, so plants in a garden must enhance the space they occupy and make the garden more beautiful by their presence. If the reason for a plant's inclusion is that the owner or gardener likes it, that is reason enough; but it must prove its value. Through form, leaves, blossoms, thrifty appearance, or other particular merit, it should be set in the place most appropriate for it, so that it can have its individuality shown up to best advantage.

Let us consider first what each plant is esteemed for. In house plants used in the garden, and in so-called foliage plants, there is the outline of the plant itself: the shape of the individual leaves, the texture, and color of those leaves. All of these characteristics make a plant attractive and usable.

FORM OR OUTLINE OF PLANTS

Plants, like people, come in all sizes and shapes. By careful pruning we keep the outlines slim or wide, tall or short, though basically, the plant (or person) has tendencies in certain directions, which cannot be ignored. *Sansevieria* has tall, pointed leaves and a pert manner of growing. No amount of pruning or shaping will turn it into a bushy form or trailing vine. Coleus and Begonias are bushy and must be kept that way to be attractive. A Dogwood tree has certain tendencies toward a horizontal branch-growth which is beautifully artistic. Judicious pruning of suckers and other branches will encourage these artistic outlines, but not change them. The natural growth for Sweet Alyssum is a low bushy form, somewhat tumbling. We can keep this cut back to improve the shape, but no amount of pruning can actually give it other than a shrubby rounded form.

In the use of foliage plants in shady garden-areas, the attention paid to the form and other individual characteristics of plants should be almost as strict as in landscaping so that we can make the best use of the plant. The fundamental principles of design are the same. Tall, pointed plants (like *Sansevierias*) are dominant features, or focal points, in a planting. In flower arrangement, the focal point is usually a rounded form buttoning up the arrangement where flowers meet container. In landscaping, the focal point catches the eye from a distance. It is the feature toward which all other planting leads. Build down from these dominant features or focal points through the bushy forms of foliage plants, or through the naked stemmed plants such as *Caladiums,* which add interest but need something even lower to tie the arrangement to the ground.

Clumps of mints can be pruned to bushy forms, and make practical as well as lovely additions to the shady garden. Their tendency to grow rampantly must be curbed before they become too leggy. Keep them in bounds or your garden-area will be discouragingly overrun.

Hostas are included here, because their foliage is so much more important than most of the blossoms. They have a fountain-like manner of growing — each leaf from the root — that is almost too distinctive for use as a bushy or filler plant, though it is excellent as a cover-up for bare stems. If you have

(Gottscho-Schleisner)

A judicious grouping of *Hosta ventricosa*
with the shrub behind it.

trouble with the lower leaves of phlox, plant a *Hosta* in front and never mind the naked phlox stems. Used as accents, *Hostas* are excellent beside a rock or bit of old stump, at either side of a walk, or at a corner. Like a "period" in writing, they give a finish to certain questionable areas.

SHAPES OF THE LEAVES

Leaves offer a variety of outlines. Plants belonging to the same plant family often have similar characteristics so that one can guess to which family a plant belongs merely by looking at its leaves. Bunchberry, for instance, is similar in foliage to Dogwood. Further investigation shows you that it *is* a dogwood *(Cornus canadensis),* though growing only about 6 inches in height. Rounded tri-foliate foliage would certainly suggest a legume, a Clover, or some kind of Pea.

Hosta leaves come in a variety of sizes and a variation of shapes from enormous, snub-nosed, rounded forms to lance-shaped leaves of 3–4 inches. There is a characteristic "Hosta-look" to all of them. Yucca leaves are stiff and pointed; Iris leaves are flat and sword-like, also pointed; Day-lilies have long, grass-like leaves. Leaves of *Heuchera* are irregularly lobed. Wild Ginger has heart-shaped leaves. And so it goes, with leaves of many descriptions, some of them so fantastic that we need only to imagine the wildest shape and hunt long enough, to find a leaf to correspond. Our job in the garden, particularly where we have a lot of shade, is to arrange our plants so that the foliage of each is either played up, or helps play up other more interesting foliage.

As we become acquainted with individual plants, we find we pass some by quickly, probably because the bush, tree, or perennial has nothing that commands our attention. *Lonicera*

is an uninteresting shrub when it has neither flower nor berry
to decorate it. Its form is rounded, its leaves similar to hundreds of other leaves. Even its blossoms are not spectacular,
although there are some varieties with quite lovely blossoms.
Its chief virtue lies in the decorative red berries that attract
the birds. For yard interest it makes a good shield in a protective or screen planting, and it can be used as a filler-plant.
On the other hand, the little Japanese Maple *(Acer palmatum)* in its red and purple-foliaged varieties, and with leaves
so deeply cleft they are reminiscent of fingers, immediately
commands attention. The leaves of *Caladium* like others of
the Arum Family resemble arrow heads in outline and would
be striking even if they did not come in a gorgeous array of
colors. The Castor-Bean *(Ricinus communis)* whose enormous
leaves are divided into from 5–11 lobes, is an arresting plant
from its very size.

TEXTURE OF LEAVES

Often it is difficult to know why certain plant combinations appeal to us. In an arrangement some flowers seem more
artistic used with foliage other than their own. Why is the
combination of one set of leaves so much more appealing than
another set? Frequently, it has something to do with texture.
Texture is the feel of anything — that innate, indescribable
quality that comes only with continual appreciation and
study. It belongs to seeing and knowing, as well as to feeling.

The leaves and blossoms of our plants also have different
textures. One leaf is thin; another, thick and substantial
looking. Leaves like those of *Epimedium* are delicate and wiry
in appearance. Placed next to other delicate wiry foliage, like
that of Maidenhair Fern, they do not show up to best advan-

tage. It would be a better contrast to have *Epimedium* next to one of the smaller Hostas, with leaves of a more substantial texture. Leaves of *Stachys lanata* suggest the common name of Wooly Lamb's Ears, for they are thick, soft, and as velvety as the ears of baby lambs. Mullein leaves are gray and somewhat similar in texture — too similar for the two plants to be used together.

The next time you are in the garden, pick a few leaves and study them. Are they rough, hairy, smooth, thin, thick? Try to compare them to the texture of various plant materials with which you are familiar, then close your eyes and try to identify a few of the outstanding examples by their texture. Open your eyes and try combining different kinds of leaves and note the difference that textures make.

COLOR OF LEAVES

Color, in leaves as well as in blossoms, makes the most spectacular contribution to a garden's beauty. To many people color *is* a garden, but when gardening in the shade, one learns to appreciate the less flamboyant colors, and the playing up of one color against another, of one tint or shade against another, and the use of certain colors to make dramatic emphasis in the design of a garden.

If one asks casually what color is a leaf, the answer is invariably "green," but what shade and tone of green? They range from the creamy white tints of leaves such as *Hosta variegata* to the deep greens of some of the Yews. A variety of *Chamaecyparis* is bright yellow-green. There is the blue-gray-green of *Hosta sieboldiana,* the hunter's green of the Red Pine, the pale bluish green of one of the *Impatiens* varieties.

Besides green leaves there are leaves of other colors.

A pale pink *Begonia semperflorens* blooming
at the feet of tall Blue Lobelia.

Hosta fortunei virdis marginata unfolds a beautiful brilliant lime-green edged with deeper olive-green. Some of the leaves of the Calla-Lily begonia are pure white. The new growth of Japanese *andromeda* is pink and sometimes a bright bronze red, as well as being of exquisite form and texture.

We have mentioned the two red-leafed Maples, but do you know the Purple Beeches? Many Blueberry leaves are often red or green tinged with red. Croton leaves are a combination of green and yellow. Coleus comes in various shades of red with touches of red and green. There are three *Hostas* with green leaves edged with white, and *Caladium* leaves in various bright color combinations. These unusual and interesting leaves should be dramatized, or set against an all-green background where they will stand out in the designs of garden-pictures.

But how are we to tell where a plant will stand out? The answer is simple. When you buy a tree or a shrub, balled and burlapped from the nursery, stand it where you think it would look well and study it from all angles. Consider the form of the plant, the shapes of the leaves as compared to those of neighboring plants. There should be good contrast, the plant should fit into the territory meant for it, and do the job intended. If it is a filler-plant, it should close a gap in a border or give privacy. Perhaps it is a large well-shaped evergreen shrub to hide a blemish in a tree trunk. If so, its foliage should be adequate and substantial enough against the rough texture of the tree trunk. If it is to be green foliage or next to green foliage, try to have contrast in form, texture, or shade of green.

When you set out your house plants for the summer, place them where they will fit into your garden-picture. If you need a low shrubby plant for an empty space, that is the spot for

(Courtesy H. A. Zager)

Plants like *Hosta decorata* and *H. fortunei* are
important for their foliage to a shady garden.

your largest *Begonia semperflorens.* If you have a dim corner
that you want to bring to life, use it for Coleus or Rabbit's
Foot Fern. In lightly shaded areas Patience plants in their
varieties will grow luxuriantly and bloom the entire summer.

Foliage counts for much in the shady garden. Take time

to study the various types. Learn to appreciate the different characteristics.

Foliage and House Plants That Like Shade

Acorus — Hardy, herbaceous water-loving plants. Good for shady pool. Can be grown in dryer locations. Grass-like foliage. *A. gramineus* var. *variegatus* has interesting white-striped leaves and is often planted in urns.

Aglaonema — Chinese Evergreen. Grows in water or soil. Excellent for tucking in an unused spot beside a shady pool, or in the pool itself. Will live under the densest branches in rich compost for the summer.

Allium — Chives. To 10″. Onion Family. Good — and useful edging to small shady garden. Shear tops for use and to keep from straggly growth.

Anthericum — Spider Plant. Fountain of grass-like leaves. Popular and easy houseplant. Will live out of doors in a mild climate. *A. Bichetii* with variegated leaves, most commonly seen. Attractive tucked in with pool planting. Sometimes surprises you with spikes of fragrant white blossoms.

Aspidistra — Old-fashioned houseplant coming back into favor for flower arrangements. Leaves: stiff, glossy, evergreen. Effective on shady terraces, in pots. Grows luxuriantly out of doors in the far South.

Begonia — The *Rhizomatous* begonias include the Rex hybrids, grown mostly for interesting and unusual foliage. Some with long sprays of lovely blossoms. Good potted plants for terraces. Fibrous-rooted Begonias are those usually grown for their prodigious bloom. The variety *B. semperflorens,* and its numerous hybrids, are excellent bedding plants. Easily ground-rooted.

Billbergia — Epiphytes or air-plants. Pineapple Family, resembling tops of pineapples. *B. nutans* an excellent houseplant with spectacular flower. Set in the garden in summer as a contrasting note to viney foliage. In fall repot offshoots only.

Bryophyllum — Fleshy perennials of the Figwort Family. Scalloped fleshy leaves which develop little new plants in each of the scallops. In the garden, plant in rock walls among crevices.

Caladium — Ornamental, heart-shaped foliage with veined and marbled effects in brilliant colors. Start indoors in the North from tubers. In South, rest bulbs between growing periods.

Calathea — Maranta Family and closely allied with *Maranta*. Interestingly marked leaves. Needs good drainage, leaf mould, shade, and a warm atmosphere. In the South, grown in shade. Should not be set out even in summer, any farther North than New York.

Cissus rhombifolia — Grape Ivy. Leaves glossy and 3-foliolate. Popular house plant. If protected from wind, it can be set out of doors around a shaded pool, as a summer ground cover, or to fill in where a low shrubby vine is needed. In fall bring in whole plant or nip off ends of branches to use in water.

Codiaeum — Crotons. Brilliantly colored and variegated leaves. Need some shade. In the North can be used in sun or partial shade, the more sun, the more variation and brilliance in the colors.

Comptonia — See Chapter 9.

Cordyline — Pot-plant resembling *Dracaena*. Leaves often with suffusion of colors, particularly in older plants. Light rich soil and warmth. Light frost will not kill them, but consistently cool weather slows down their growth.

Cornus alba argenteo-marginata — Variegated Dogwood. Green leaves edged with white. Beautiful addition to the shady garden. Give plenty of compost. Treat as other Dogwoods.

Dracaena — House plant easily grown in light rich soil. Needs light, but not sun. Easily propagated. Glossy, bright-colored foliage.

Fittonia — Tropical. In the South, excellent plants for growing under benches and in other dark corners. *F. argyroneura* has velvety green leaves netted with white. Well-drained loamy leafmold. Roots easily.

Geonoma — A palm that is a natural undergrowth for its native South American mountains. Most attractive in smaller sizes. Gives a touch of the exotic to the outdoor shady garden, useful for shady terraces.

Helxine Soleiroli — Babys-Tears. Tiny bright green leaves. Covers a pot in no time. Excellent ground-cover for light shaded places. Does not like frost.

Hosta — Fleshy rooted plants of the Lily Family hailing originally from China and Japan. Leaves, prominently ribbed, grow singly from roots; make beautiful mounds of foliage that increase and grow more beautiful with age. Genus contains some of the most interesting foliage plants. All tolerate shady conditions and most varieties prefer the shade. They are at their best in gravelly soil, rich in compost, but they will grow practically anywhere. Most of the flowers are fairly attractive, but foliage is what counts. Particularly good for flower arrangements. Plants make good accents for corners, borders, or fillers. A few of the more spectacular and interesting:

> *Hosta caerulea* — Blue Plaintain-Lily. Large glossy dark green leaves on sturdy leaf stems up to 18″. Old clumps grow huge. If desired, limit plant in its early years by keeping only a few roots growing. Flower-bells, bluest of any hostas, crowded along the stalk.
> *H. Sieboldiana* — Huge heart-shaped leaves of a grayish cast. Outstandingly beautiful. Flowers, very pale lavender.
> *H. undulata variegata* and *H. undulata univitatta* — Green and white twisted and curled foliage, ideal for arrangements. Excellent in the shade.

H. fortunei albo-marginata — Pointed, pert leaves of deep green edged with white. Two other white-edged varieties. *H. minor alba* — Small fountains of pointed leaves to 8″. Fine for the shady rock garden. Flowers — sweet little white bells standing well out from the flower stem.

Hydrophyllum — Water-Leaf. To 2′. Large lobed, palm-shaped leaves. Good for dressing up the lower parts of shrubs or small trees in rich soil with plenty of compost.

Impatiens Sultani — Patience Plant. One of best plants to set out in the semi-shaded garden. Makes small bushy foliage plants studded with bright blossoms practically all summer. Blossoms in variety, from orange-red to lovely pink. Make cuttings in March–April for summer. Susceptible to frost.

Maranta bicolor — Prayer Plant. Popular houseplant. Can be set out of doors when very warm. Leaves with brownish splotches along the central vein. Likes moisture; compost; do not press soil too firmly about their roots.

Melissa officinalis — Lemon Balm. Aromatic sweet herb of the Mint Family. Shiny leaves smell and taste of lemon. Keep pinching back to keep from getting too leggy.

Mentha — Mint. Varieties make good clumps of foliage for difficult shady places. Keep pinched back. Varieties hybridize freely. *M. Requienii,* creeping, can be used as a ground-cover. *M. Pulegium* — Pennyroyal. Gives the effect of creeping, but is a tumbler, liking rocks and old stumps. It is said to keep mosquitoes away. In the fall, a root potted and taken into the house grows attractively down over the sides of the pot. *M. rotundifolia* — Apple Mint. Furry gray-green leaves good contrast to other greens.

Palms — Many varieties which make good house plants. With-stand shade and dry house conditions. A few grow out of doors in the South. In the North, set them on shady terraces and porches during the summer. Like a sandy soil enriched with manure. They do not like too large pots, nor sudden blasts of cold wind.

Petroselinum — Parsley. A biennial herb grown as an annual. Attractive. Useful. Sun or shade. Ideal border for a small herb garden or a difficult shady spot. Pinch back flower stalks the second year to keep the plant bushy, letting a few go to seed and come the next year.

Philodendron — Many varieties grown out of doors in the South. A house plant in the North; it loves being set out in the summer, and drapes over shaded rocks or around a pool. Loves compost of fibrous loam and leafmold.

Physalis alkekengi — Chinese lanterns. Grown principally for bright, decorative red "lanterns" which are dried and used in winter. Will thrive anywhere, but must be kept in check.

Sedum — Sedums are naturally sun-loving, but a few do fairly well in a light shade. Leaves sparser; flowers, fewer. Some used as ground-covers. Many will seed themselves in shady places where they would not have succeeded had they been planted. Try *S. Nevi, S. sarmentosum, S. acre.* Give them leafmold in a sandy soil in a rather dry location.

Sempervivum — Houseleeks, Hens-and-Chickens. The same can be said for this genus. They are worth a try if you have a shady corner that you want filled with something interesting. Compact rosettes of fleshy leaves.

Stachys Lanata — Wooly Lambs-ears. Hardy and strong-growing. Foliage a soft downy gray, reminding one of lambs' ears. Will take a light shade.

Symphytum — Comfrey. To 3'. Old-world perennial herb with supposed healing properties. Plant grown for its foliage. Var. *officinale* and variations.

Verbascum thapsus — Common Mullein. To 7'. A biennial, growing wild in waste spaces. The first year's rosettes of soft gray leaves make lovely accents in the shady garden, and also in flower arrangements. The stalks of yellow flowers are not unattractive at the far end of a garden where they arise in stately dignity. Seed pods excellent for dried arrangements.

Yucca — Grown more for its foliage than for its spires of white blossoms. They like the sun but will do very well in shade. Excellent for holding back the soil on dry steep banks. Var. *Y. filamentosa,* or Adam's Needle grown in the North. Evergreen.

9

Ground-Covers and Vines

✧❋✧❋✧❋✧❋✧❋✧❋✧❋✧❋✧❋✧❋✧❋✧❋✧❋✧❋✧

A GROUND-COVER is a low-growing, often evergreen plant used in place of grass, pebbles, a mulching material, or earth, in a spot that might otherwise be unsightly. Many times it decorates the base of trees and shrubs to keep the roots cool and to hold in moisture. It also keeps down weeds and other plants that might spring up unbidden.

Establish a good ground-cover where it is needed, and your troubles in that area will be partly over. As most of them are to grow in the shade, plant them with plenty of compost. The following spring, add a little fertilizer and more compost, if needed; cultivate and weed in early summer. Water during dry spells and watch out for weed-demons during the warm weather. After that the ground-cover should feel at home and start looking after itself.

It goes without saying that of all ground-covers, a good green lawn is most beautiful. Nothing is more satisfactory than to kick one's feet in velvety turf, or to step across the smooth carpet of a freshly mowed "perfect" lawn. But how many "perfect" lawns are there? Where are the home-owners

136

A fine lawn contributes to the harmony
of white birches and the vista beyond.

who can afford the time and money, or both, to have every weed pulled, to repair winter ravages, to fill in the inevitable dips and hollows? It takes time to make a perfect lawn, particularly if it is under trees.

In open areas, where grass is established, see that it is cultivated, fertilized, and otherwise cared for so that it keeps in good condition. In areas where trees are thick and where a lovely lawn would not be appreciated so much as the trees, let moss or other flat growths take over. As long as there is green there, the kind of green will not matter, particularly if it is kept neatly raked and edged.

In parts of the South, where grass does not grow well, grass-like substitutes are used, such as *Mondo japonicum, Meibomia,* and *Liriope spicata,* or low-growing plants like *Dichondra.* Most of these do not like being walked on, but they take quite a lot of abuse and give a good appearance in general. In northern shady areas, where it is the trees that matter, a carpet of something like *Veronica officinalis* might be used. Under Pine trees, the ground beneath can be carpeted with pine needles, which give a resilient walking surface and a neat appearance. In sandy districts, I've seen whole yards covered this way, with only the flower beds and borders — arranged artistically in certain areas — to add green to the picture. It is effective, practical, and charming.

Vines and shallow-rooting plants make the best living ground-covers around the base of trees whose roots tend to grow toward the top of the soil. Pachysandra grows under a Beech where grass refuses to grow because of so many tree-roots. Woodbine, Ivy, or other viney plants grow under low-hanging Maple boughs. Plant the vines under the outside tips of the branches where roots are fewer. Train them inward, toward the trunk, to make a carpet.

Ground-covers, correctly used, add much to the practical garden picture. Pachysandra or Periwinkle, planted around and among foundation shrubs not only looks attractive, but eliminates the need for mulching with peat moss every year. These rooting trailers act as a much and stay green all winter. Ground-covers planted along the edges of foundations help tie the building to the ground. In the North, Woodbine and Ivy are loved for this reason and because they will creep up the side of a house and chimney. In the South, Strawberry Geranium and *Pilea microphylla* are used a great deal in foundation planting.

On the north side of a house, where flowering shrubs and perennials are apt to be unhappy, Lily-of-the-Valley, as a ground-cover, gives green all summer and sprays of dainty fragrant blossoms in spring. For outside cellar window-wells in shade, plant Kenilworth Ivy or *Akebia quinata* to trail down the sides of the well without shutting out the light. Where there are steps to a house and a bit of banking that might become muddy in rainy weather, consider one of the creeping Junipers *(Juniperus horizontalis)* which will take a light shade, or *Euonymous radicans*. Steeper banks, or stretches of shady areas under trees or bushes, can be planted to Fragrant Sumac or Yellow Root. (See Chapter 10.) If you want a glamorous ground-cover, try *Pachistima canbyi*, which is evergreen, and grows to 1'; it turns a beautiful bronze in the autumn. A few rocks placed at strategic spots in a banking will hold back the soil, too, and can be interspersed with groups of shade-loving plants of varying heights to create the semblance of a shady rock garden. Low-growing ground-covers, if needed, can be planted between the groups.

Flagstone walks and terraces call for a flat type of ground-cover. Here, rosettes of *Ajuga, Phlox stolonifera,* or *Anten-*

Ageratum makes an interesting and attractive
ground cover around flagstones.

naria plantaginifolia make themselves at home, if not too often trampled under heel. In gardens with natural outcroppings of rock-ledges the creeping type of ground-cover is excellent in contrast to some of the upright rock-plants, and also to enhance the ledge. *Arabis* makes lovely silvery mats of leaves during the summer, to tumble down over a rock, if the shade is not too dense.

Vines serve climbing purposes as well, and can be a natural means of relating the house to the ground. What chimney is not further enhanced by hardy Ivy or Virginia Creeper, which turns a beautiful red in the fall? A quick-growing plant for the side of a house, is Boston Ivy *(Parthenocissus tricuspidata)* with large, lustrous deciduous leaves that have brilliant fall color.

There are all sorts of other uses for vines: to screen porches or breezeways, to climb trellises, arbors, over summer houses, or small tool houses, around lamp posts, bird baths, old stumps—both to serve as decoration and to keep the stump damp so it will rot. Unsightly garbage cans can be hidden — or at least partially hidden — by a strong-growing vine. Bulkheads can be disguised by living greenery along the outside, but so planted that it won't interfere with usage. The compost pile can often be made a unique attraction if quick-growing vines are allowed to scramble over it.

Old stone walls were made for vines. Bittersweet can ramble over them without restraint and give you an abundance of bright berries in the bargain. It likes shade. Southern stone walls might be decorated with Carolina Yellow Jessamine, which will take a light shade, even to the point of producing some of its lovely yellow blossoms.

Never waste a fence, even in the shade! If you are crowded for space, a fence gives you more planting area be-

cause the plants grow up, not out. Two lovely fence-climbers
are *Thunbergia grandiflora* and *T. alata,* the former with
large blue flowers and the latter with appealing purple-
throated, apricot-colored flowers. Southern vines they are, but
they will easily decorate northern greenhouses in sun or partial shade, and *T. alata,* or Black-Eyed Susan is often grown
as an annual.

Strong-caned roses like Silver Moon will bloom with
as little as five hours of direct sunlight a day. Virgins Bower
(Clematis virginiana) will offer good blooms in light, or partial shade. All Clematis flowers seek the sun, but their roots
like cool refreshment, a combination which the shady garden
can often offer, particularly when a fence is involved. In a
small yard, there is nothing like a fence with a vine growing
on it, to extend the vision. One sees the vine beyond the other
plantings and it suggests expanse.

A city garden can be treated this way, one end "pushed
out" by means of a sapling fence with grape vines espaliered
against it. The bold leaves of the Grape not only will provide
contrast to dark evergreens in front of them, and to nearby
deciduous shrubbery, but give a feeling of spaciousness and
depth, of something beyond.

Some vines are used interchangeably with, and as,
ground-covers.

Confined between bricks or low metal walls sunk in the
ground, they make decorative borders for lawns and terraces.
Established in this way, with some of the low ranch-type
houses they lend a note of practical embellishment, in following a long, low line of the house. The trailing varieties are
lovely set into some of the new built-up flower beds to serve
as a ground-cover that also trails down over the sides. Other
vines must have supports to be at their best. Many vines prefer

sunshine to shade, but a surprising number tolerate shade even to the extent of giving flowers and fruits. A few (such as Ivy) grow better in shade.

GROUND–COVERS AND VINES THAT TOLERATE SHADE

Actinidia arguta — Bower *Actinidia*. High-climbing, vigorous. Glossy green leaves at end of red petioles. Good for screening purposes. Rank grower in good soil. Other species.

Adlumia fungosa — Allegheny Vine. Biennial; self-sows when established. Low and bushy the first season. Pinnate leaves with attractive, delicate leaflets. Ample panicles of white and purplish flowers. Does not like wind or direct sun.

Aegopodium podagraria — Bishops-Weed. Ground-cover to 14″. Quick-growing and weedy. Ideal for some shady places. Var. *variegatum* particularly attractive.

Ajuga — Bugle-Weed. Easily grown, flat mats of leaves. Flower spikes to 10″, in pink, blue, or white. Quick grower. Likes humus, shade. Ground-cover for untrodden places. Purple and variegated varieties.

Akebia quinata. Light, airy vine to 30′. Good for arbors, waterspouts, posts, etc. Neat. As a ground-cover, kills other plants. Dark-colored flowers need hand pollination for fruit.

Ampelopsis brevipedunculata — Porcelain-Berry. Vigorous climber with deeply-lobed leaves. Climbs or sprawls but should be where its beautiful fruit (pale-lilac to turquoise) can be appreciated. Not particular as to soil.

Antennaria — Pussys-Toes. Not usually at nurseries, but plentiful in the fields. Excellent mat for between stepping stones. Poor soil. Tolerates shade.

Arenaria montana — Mountain sandwort. Flat mats. Does not like to be stepped on. Pretty white flowers. Sandy soil with humus, so that water drains quickly. Light and half-shade.

Aristolochia durior — Dutchmans-Pipe. Vine to 30′. Native. Hardy. Tolerant of shade and dry soil, but likes rich soil. Large, heart-shaped leaves, making dense screen. Flowers — odd little purplish "pipes."

Asarum canadense — Wild Ginger. Ground-cover for shady, woodsy places with plenty of humus.

Celastrus scandens — Bitter-Sweet. Grows almost anywhere. Shade, as well as sun. If near a building, must be pruned heavily. Unsurpassed for old stone walls, trellises, difficult places. Beautiful red and yellow berries in the fall. Must have two sexes.

Cerastium — Snow-in-Summer. Mats of Silvery white foliage. White starry flowers in spring. Tolerates light shade.

Clematis paniculata — Autumn Clematis. Delicate, graceful habit, growing in dense masses on fences, etc., but not a dense climber. Airy blossoms. Many hybrids, most of which like cool roots, but need sun for bloom. Try light shade, and experiment. Rich soil, moisture, lime.

Convalleria majalis — Lily-of-the-Valley. Excellent ground-cover for shady places. Grows anywhere. Delightfully fragrant white blossoms in spring. Good foliage all summer. Red berries.

Cymbalaria muralis (Linaria cymbalaria) — Kenilworth Ivy. Not quite hardy, but seeds itself. Likes moisture and shade. Ground-cover or dainty trailer. Lilac flowers. Excellent for small places.

Dolichos Hosei — Sarawak-Bean. Trailing legume, covering ground to 6″ in several months. Grown in South, mostly in shady locations. Good for broad banks, slopes, orchards. Can be walked on a little.

Euonymous radicans and varieties. Wintercreeper. Trailing evergreen; sometimes pruned to shrubby formation (as in a hedge). Very useful and ornamental; around steps, old walls, over rocks. Low or shrubby. (See local catalogues.)

Ficus radicans. More suitable as southern ground-cover than *F. pumila.* Establishes easily, enduring temperatures to 26°. Does well in shade, rather moist, heavy soil.

Fragaria chiloensis — Strawberry. Grows in shade if berries are not wanted. Weed out old plants.

Gelsemium sempervirens — Carolina Yellow Jessamine. Twining evergreen shrub for slopes, banks, or other large areas. Fragrant large yellow flowers; less profuse in shade; acid soil; part-shade.

Hedera Helix — English Ivy. Glossy evergreen leaves, usually lobed, often with attractive white veining. Excellent for ground-cover, or as a vine. Good for cutting. Var. *Baltica* hardier in New England. Comes through Winter better in shade. Pine boughs to keep leaves from burning. Many uses; many varieties. *H. canariensis* — Algerian or Canary Island Ivy; used in Southern states.

Hydrangea petiolaris — Climbing Hydrangea. Clinging vine to 75′. Flat, white clusters of flowers 6–10″ across. Brick walls, or a tree, rather than wood. Slow to get established, but worth cultivating.

Iris cristata — Ground-cover for certain places. Takes an almost dense shade, and blooms. Excellent.

Juniperus horizontalis —Creeping Juniper. To 12″. For bank, or large, shady area, plant 2′ apart in staggered rows. Eventually grow into each other.

Lamium maculatum — Dead-Needle. To 1′. White striped leaves make an interesting and attractive ground-cover. Flowers add white or rosy purple color. Easy to grow.

Lathyrus latifolius — Everlasting Pea. Rose-flowering. Easily cultivated, thriving almost anywhere. Rampant grower; good for trellises, walls, wild, rough places. A natural shade-lover. Var. White Pearl, and others.

Liriope spicata — Creeping Liriope. Lilyturf. Grass-like ever-green to 10″. Half to full shade, replacing grass in many places. Good or poor soil. Drought-resistant, hardy. Purple to white flowers in late summer. Excellent ground-cover.

Lonicera henryi — Henry's Honeysuckle. Half-evergreen, ac-tually a climbing shrub. Fragrant white flowers changing to yellow. Many uses. Good for covering sloping banks, old stumps, rocks, can be trained to a trellis, but strictly pruned. Takes light shade.

Lysimachia nummularia — Moneywort. Excellent ground-cover for right places. Withstands shade. Flat round leaves, pretty little yellow flowers. Likes rich soil.

Meibomia cana — Tick-trefoil. Procumbent, woody perennial. Sun or shade. Needs to be mowed more in shade, as it com-pletely takes over like a lawn. Light, well-drained soil. En-dures tramping.

Mentha pulegium — Pennyroyal. Flat, creeping herb with aromatic scent. Said to keep mosquitoes away. Light shade.

Mitchella repens — Partridge-Berry. Native evergreen. Not used nearly enough. Small, round leaves, white-veined. Small, white flowers followed by prominent red berry. Needs acid soil, compost, and shade.

Nepeta hederacea — Ground Ivy. Creeping, mat-forming per-ennial, for sun or shade. Light blue flowers in sparse clusters. Apt to be weedy unless restricted. Lovely variegated variety.

Ophiopogon japonicus — Dwarf Lily-turf. Dark-green, grass-like leaves up to 12″. Flowers small, lilac-colored, usually hid-den by foliage. Dwarfer but less enduring than *Liriope*. Ground-cover in South; sun or shade.

Pachistima Canbyi. Evergreen to 12″. One of best winter-green ground-covers. Acid soil and shade. Small leaves turn beautiful bronze in fall.

Pachysandra terminalis — Japanese Spurge. Another excellent ground-cover. Evergreen. Attractive for around shrubs and base of trees. Likes compost and shade.

Parthenocissus quinquefolia — Virginia Creeper. Deciduous, high-climbing vine. Clings to walls and trees. Excellent for banks. Beautiful fall coloring. Handsome, glossy, 5-parted leaves.

Parthenocissus tricuspidata — Boston Ivy. High-climbing. Trifoliate leaves. Glossy. Dense, flat covering for walls. Brilliant yellow and red fall coloring. Other species stand part-shade too.

Phlox stolonifera — Creeping Phlox. Flat, half-evergreen mats of leaves. Beautiful orchid-colored phlox-like flowers in spring. Delightfully fragrant. Loves humus; easily grown.

Pilea microphylla — Artillery Plant. Leaves dark green. Good ground-cover for Southern states; also used for edging. *P. nummulariaefolia.*

Polygonum Auberti — Silver Lace-Vine. Fast-grower to 25′. Long clusters of greenish white flowers in late summer. Fragrant. Takes light shade only.

Saxifraga sarmentosa — Strawberry-Geranium. Interesting, green, veined leaves, reddish below. Creeps by numerous stolons to form good ground-cover for southern gardens. Prefers shade. Northern house plant.

Schizocentron elegans — Mexican creeping vine. Forms thick carpets. Charming plant. Deep blue flowers. Shade or sun; light warm soil; mild climate, but can be grown in New York.

Sedum acre. This and other species and varieties will take light shade, and such is their "running" capacity that they make good ground-covers for certain areas. Some are evergreen; seed readily, and can be moved around without suffering.

Thunbergia grandiflora. Tall climber. Large beautiful tubular blue flowers. Tender. Good for fences in semi-shade. *T.*

alata — Black-eyed Susan. Climbs trees, fences, etc. Delightful apricot-colored flowers with dark throats. Grown in the North as an annual. Likes sun but will take partial shade.

Thymus — Thyme. Many varieties. Likes sun but takes a light shade. Good for between stepping stones. Forms flat mat.

Trachelospermum jasminoides — Star Jasmine. Fragrant, white flowers in small clusters. Dark green, evergreen foliage. Rapid growth to make a thick screen. Likes humus and moist shade.

Veronica officinalis — Common Speedwell. Matted, creeping evergreen. Native. Grows under trees and in shade where no grass will grow. Excellent for around such things as lilacs.

Vinca minor — Periwinkle. Favorite trailing evergreen ground-cover. Glossy leaves. Attractive violet-blue flowers. Hardy. Likes humus. One of best plants to grow under trees.

Vitis — Grape. Fast-growing, deciduous vine. Coarse, but attractive leaves, particularly when young. Vine as ornamental as it is useful. Takes an almost dense shade. Japanese beetles infest them.

10

Deciduous Shrubs Tolerant of Shade

✣❀✣❀✣❀✣❀✣❀✣❀✣❀✣❀✣❀✣❀✣❀✣❀✣❀✣❀✣❀✣❀✣

PLANT A TREE or shrub in your yard and your whole outlook is changed. A shrub can shut you away from prying eyes of passing motorists or curious neighbors. It can help shield the clothesyard or hide the garbage can. A shrub might serve as a focal point at the end of a path, or stand as sentinel at the beginning of a driveway. It can soften the edges of build-ings or make a picture to be enjoyed through a window. It can be a nesting place for birds, and serve complete bird meals with berries or nuts.

In the shady garden a deciduous shrub can be a fascinat-ing study through the whole year. The Dogwoods, for in-stance, are four-season shrubs or small trees, blooming more abundantly the more sun they receive, but giving us many blossoms even in shaded areas. In winter they offer interesting outlines; with the branches of the red-twigged Dogwoods brightly colorful against evergreens or a light colored house.

(C. A. Horn)

Deciduous Shrubs can help shield the clothesyard.

Also, on warm winter days, come the early Witch-Hazel (*Hamamelis vernalis*) blooms, little yellow bunches of string along the branches. There are swelling Forsythia buds that can be brought indoors and forced into bloom. Soon the February Daphne *(D. Mesereum)* is aglow with fragrant lilac-purple flowers.

Spring is heralded in many parts of the country by white clouds of Shadblow in the woods, or at the edges of shady shrub borders. Spicebush and Cornelian Cherry tree, a Dogwood *(Cornus mas)* are outlined in yellow. In lightly shaded areas the little round bumps along the branches of Flowering Quince take color. Forsythia buds swell to the bursting point. Spring has come.

All summer Forsythia makes a good background shrub for our shaded areas. Its foliage is good and can be used for cutting. Some of the Bush-Honeysuckles, which stand shade, are bright with red berries beloved by birds. The cornelian Cherry Tree has large lush red berries, like Christmas tree ornaments among the green. Some shade-loving shrubs, like *Clethra,* have their blooming period in summer. At a time when few other plants are in bloom it is covered with upright spikes of white fragrant blossoms.

Shady gardens in fall can still be colorful. Shrubs and trees, well chosen, carry interest through September and October. Then, as yellow leaves come sifting down, our native Witch-Hazel *(Hamamelis virginiana),* which stands a deeper shade than Asiatic varieties, comes into its own. Little yellow blossoms along bare branches, which call to our attention the artistic outlines of this shrub. It is not used nearly enough in American gardens.

In choosing a deciduous shrub — as in choosing any plant — decide the purpose it is to serve. Do you want it for height,

Ferns dress up rough edges of a garden.

for bushiness, for flowers, for the birds? Is your plot small, and must you therefore choose something with as much interest as possible? Or do you have room enough to plant a variety and so can try the unusual?

For easy success, you would do well to stick to those plants which are native, or at least, hardy in your vicinity. Make a study of what grows easily. Books and lists can only suggest, for even in the same zone, locations *of* gardens and *in* gardens make a difference. A Redbud is hardy in New England, but set in the open where it can be buffeted by the wind, it will not be happy. Like Dogwoods and some of the deciduous Azaleas, it grows with trees that give protection from winter winds and hot sun.

If you like to hurry spring in your shady areas choose shrubs that offer bloom before leaves, such as the early Witch-Hazels and Dogwoods. If you like something unusual, try *Fothergilla* with its brush-like blossoms, or Flowering Raspberry with large bold exotic leaves and continuous bloom. If you want something for the birds, choose some of the Viburnums, Honeysuckles, or Shadbush. If you know you have an acid soil choose blueberries and *Clethra,* which must have an acid soil. Many shrubs will grow in any kind of soil as long as they have an abundance of humus and organic materials; others must have the right proportion of iron that an acid soil gives them. Still others prefer an alkaline soil.

The personal characteristics of a shrub or small tree should partly determine where it is to go. If you want a winter-blooming Witch-Hazel so you can enjoy the blossoms in January, or a February Daphne, don't plant them at the extreme end of your lot where they will not be seen from your windows. If you want Pussy Willow or Forsythia so that you can cut the branches in February, don't plant them down behind the garage, beyond reach when the snow is on the ground. Do not plan your exotic or expensive shrubs for accessible locations where the neighbors' pets and children may ruin them.

The best time to move a shrub is when it is dormant which is usually in the winter. This is a plant's natural resting period. In the North, climatic conditions provide longer rest periods than in the South, dormancy beginning in November or earlier and usually lasting until spring.

From a nursery deciduous shrubs are sent with bare roots wrapped in wet moss or other material. Do not allow those roots to dry out! Dig a hole deeper than and wider than the root spread. Mix the soil at the bottom and sides with decomposed organic material from the compost pile, or with well-rotted manure, or a mixture of both. Add an inch or two of the best soil you have available, and set the bottom of the roots on that. Spread out the roots so that they are not cramped. Cover them with good soil, packed down firmly against them. If the roots spread out like a tent as rose-roots do, build a tent of soil under them. When all roots are well covered with soil, step on them to firm the soil against the roots so that there will be no air-pockets. Water well. Mix more organic material in around the outside edges of the roots. Add a little soil, then more organic material, until the hole is filled within an inch of the top. If the plant is not an acid-loving plant, sprinkle a little bone meal in with the compost material, which, incidentally, does not have to be fully decomposed to be used. Around shrubs and large plants where there are no fine roots to consider, the previous year's compost pile is about right.

If you are planting a small tree, stake it in three places. Use a piece of old rubber hose around the trunk under string

Dogwood blooms in the shade, and
tulips and pansies beneath it.

or wire so the bark won't be scraped. Weight soil around trees
or shrubs with several stones over the roots to hold them in
place. Later, when the tree or shrub is established, the stones
may be replaced with a little more soil and a good mulching
material. A slight "saucer" is left at the top of the soil to
catch and hold extra water during the first season until the
shrub gets established in its new home.

In transplanting a shrub or small tree in the same yard,
or in buying a shrub from a nearby nursery where soil is left
on the roots, much the same principles apply. The transplanting should be maneuvered in as short a time as possible,
however, with the roots remaining at all times covered with
soil, or at least kept damp, or puddled. If shrubs must go
unplanted for several days, set them in the shade and keep the
roots covered with soil.

The best time for transplanting anything is on a misty
day or just after a rain. If the ground is dry, it should have
a thorough saturation during the planting operation and
during dry spells that may occur any time the following two
seasons. If you have set in shrubs in the spring, watch them
particularly during the first summer. See that they are well-
watered in the fall before freezing weather sets in.

Although a few deciduous shrubs such as *Clethra,* Witch-
Hazel, and some Azaleas grow and bloom naturally in the
shade, the great majority have more blossoms if planted in
direct sunlight or at least where they receive a few hours of
sun each day. Many of them will endure a light patterned
shade, or as little as five hours of direct sunlight a day, and
remain thrifty enough to offer a goodly number of flowers. In
the shade, the bloom is often later and deeper in color, and
the individual flowers are larger. If you have a shady garden,
the best thing to do is to experiment with various plants in
various situations.

DECIDUOUS SHRUBS THAT TOLERATE SHADE

Acanthopanax Sieboldianus — Five-leaved *Aralia*. To 9'. Grown for its attractive five-fingered foliage. Good for flower arranging. Grows well under trees in quite a dense shade and is always neat appearing. Good hedge plant but beauty of form is lost when sheared.

Acer spicatum — To 25', usually lower. Mountain Maple. Grows well under high trees. Fall coloring scarlet and gold. *A. ginnala.* Dense shrub or small tree with bright red fruits in summer. Brilliant fall coloring. Little care.

Aesculus parviflora — Bottlebrush Buckeye. 8–12'. Large, pyramidal clusters of white blossoms in summer. The more sun, the more blossoms, but does beautifully under high trees with good air-circulation. Hardy North to Boston.

Alnus — Alders. Catkins interesting. Mostly for wet places in shady areas.

Amelanchier — Shadbush. To 20', but usually shrubby. Grows in woods but blooms better in light shade. Racemes of white blossoms as downy leaves unfold.

Aronia — Chokeberry. 3–12'. Overlooked in the woods, but an attractive shrub given room, air, and better soil. White flowers, berries, and foliage all definite assets to light woodland or naturalistic borders.

Azalea — Deciduous Rhododendron. Magnificent colors of blossoms, giving big displays at blooming time. Easily grown in right soil — acid, plenty of oak-leaf humus. Likes mulching.

Berberis — Barberry. Thorny shrub to 10'. Useful and ornamental. Most of them have yellow flowers and conspicuous red berries in the fall. Fall coloring of some varieties is unsurpassed. Unfortunately *B. vulgaris* (Common Barberry) is host to a wheat rust and should not be planted in wheat-growing regions. Japanese Barberry (*B. thunbergii*) may be used safely. Several interesting varieties — including red-foliaged *B. thunbergii atropurpurea.* Lesser known varieties are most interesting. All take quite a lot of shade *and* sun.

Benzoin aestivalis (Lindera Benzoin) — Spice-Bush. To 15′. Dense, well-shaped bush if not crowded. Greenish yellow flowers in early spring before the leaves. Large spicy leaves turn yellow in the fall. Red fruits. Takes dense shade, but has more flowers and fruits in light and partial shade. Should be better known.

Calycanthus floridus — Sweet-Shrub. To 9′. Attractive. Well-shaped. Hardy. Interesting reddish brown flowers, spicy and fragrant. Takes quite a dense shade and grows well in any soil.

Cephalanthus occidentalis — Button-Bush. 3–10′. Shrubby, rather coarse foliaged bush growing in wet ground. Adapted to gardens where humus and moisture are retained. Densely packed white flower heads are like round buttons. Light shade.

Cercis canadensis — Redbud. Small tree. Showy in early spring when branches are outlined with profusion of rosy pink flowers before the leaves come out. Handsome heart-shaped foliage. Rich, sandy, rather moist loam. Transplant when young.

Chaenomeles japonica — Dwarf Japanese Quince. To 3′. Confusion in names. This species seems to be the lower growing type of Flowering Quince. Flowers reddish scarlet. Leaves glossy; young leaves pinkish cast. Forces easily. Loves humus. Less flowers in shade but foliage is lovelier. *C. lagenaria* — Flowering Quince. Taller. (According to Donald Wyman of the Arnold Arboretum.) Many varieties, with blossoms shading from white through pinks and reds.

Clethra alnifolia — Sweet Pepperbush. Native shrub to 10′. Should be used more in home-plantings. Neat upright shrub growing by suckers. Leaves glossy. Flowers, white spikes in midsummer, fragrant. Likes humus and (probably) an acid soil. Fine for flower arrangement. If grown too dry, apt to get red spider. Hardy.

Comptonia asplenifolia — Sweet-Fern. Sweet-smelling shrub to 5'. Native. Excellent as high ground-cover for dry, barren banks. Likes sun, but tolerates shade. Difficult to transplant. Best in early spring with as large a clump of earth and roots as possible.

Cornus florida — White Flowering Dogwood. Shrubby small tree. Grows in woods, but the more sun it has, the more blossoms. Grows well with oaks and pines. Spectacular white "flowers" (really bracts) before the leaves. Showy red berries in summer. Beautiful fall coloring, as well as interesting winter outlines. Likes woodsy humus and prefers an acid soil, but seems to grow in any good garden soil. *C. mas* — Cornelian-cherry, another small tree. Branches outlined with yellow flowers in early spring. Red fruits. *C. alba sibirica* (Siberian Dogwood) to 10'; valued for red twigs in the winter and autumn coloring. Other shrubby dogwoods good.

Corylopsis sinensis — Chinese Winter-Hazel. To 10'. Pale yellow nodding racemes of blossoms opening even while the snow is on the ground. Fragrant. Leaves, striking. Shrub, graceful. Probably not hardy north of Philadelphia; might try in protected place. Light; rich soil; other good species.

Corylus maxima purpurea — Purple-leaved Filbert. Advertised to 10', but can be pruned to 5'. Purple leaves; deepest in bright sun; retains much of their lovely color in light shade; good contrast to other foliages.

Daphne Mezereum — February Daphne. To 4'. Rosy lilac flowers appearing before the leaves. Fragrant; neat growth; temperamental. Move when young.

Deutzia gracilis — To 3'. One of best dwarf Deutzias. Needs protection in the North. Takes quite a dense shade. Floriferous. White clusters of flowers. Other taller species take half-shade, but like light and air.

Diervilla sessilifolia — Southern Bush-Honeysuckle. To 5'. Hardy. Flowers, deep yellow, trumpet-shaped. Good for mass-ing along shady inclines to hold back soil. Grows anywhere. Spreads rapidly.

Eranthemum nervosum — Blue Sage. Excellent shrub for shady places in South and Southwest. Dark green foliage, coarse but effective. Bright-blue phlox-like flowers in winter and spring. Cut branches last well.

Euonymous alatus — Winged Euonymous. Valued for attractive spreading habit, and brilliant fall coloring. Red fruits after leaves have gone. Light shade. Other varieties.

Forsythia. Good, all-around shrub. Gay, yellow blossoms in early spring. Foliage good all summer; purply bronze in fall. Must be kept severely pruned. In shade, branches have more interesting angles.

Fothergilla major — Large Fothergilla. To 9′. Upright, pyramidal. Interesting spikes of white blossoms. Yellow and red in fall. Moist sandy loam, with plenty of compost. Other varieties.

Fuchsia magellanica. Small; shrubby. Hardy to Boston with protection. Many varieties grown out of doors in mild climates, and as summer pot plants in the North. Graceful; drooping branches, hung with dainty, pendulous blossoms in reds and purples. Acid soil, rough humus, full shade.

Hamamelis virginiana — Witch-Hazel. Beautiful, native shrub. Interesting growing habits. Yellow "string-like" blossoms in fall, followed by brown nut-like fruits in spring. Yellow fall coloring. *H. mollis* — Chinese Witch-Hazel, with fragrant yellow blossoms in late winter.

Hydrangea quercifolia — Oak-leaved Hydrangea. Dense, stoloniferous shrub with leaves like those of an Oak. Panicles of flowers, pinkish white, turning purple. Likes moisture but grows almost anywhere. This and other varieties enjoy partial shade.

Hypericum prolificum (aureum) — Shrubby St. Johnswort. 3′. Hardy. Dense, mounded shrub. Leaves, small and narrow.

Flowers, single, yellow. Sandy, rocky soil. Does not like to be dry. Partial shade.

Indigofera Kirilowii — Kirilow Indigo. 3'. Clusters of pink blossoms and leaflets like those of *Robinia hispida,* but neater grower. Likes sun, but will take light shade. A pretty shrub.

Kerria Japonica. To 8'. Green twigs interesting in winter. Single or double yellow blossoms in abundance, in spring. Hardy to Massachusetts but needs protection. Easily grown. Takes partial shade.

Kolkwitzia amabilis — Beauty-Bush. White-throated pink flowers in abundance in sun; less in light shade. Must be established before blooming. Likes shade in the South.

Lonicera tatarica — Tartarian Honeysuckle. Several varieties of this species with flowers varying from white to deep pink. Red berries that the birds love. Decorative. Takes shade but likes air and space. Other species good for light shades.

Lyonia ligustrina — He-Huckleberry. To 12'. Native to East and South. Small white flowers in racemes. Dense foliage that is well colored in the fall. Acid soil. Boggy conditions but tolerates garden soil and becomes attractive shrub.

Myrica caroliniensis. (M. pensylvanica) — Bayberry. To 8'. Aromatic leaves, dull green, almost evergreen. Attractive. Thrives in poor soil, but must be acid. Two sexes needed to insure gray berries.

Philadelphus coronarius — Sweet Mock-Orange. Single white, fragrant flowers in June. Strong grower and will stand aridity and some shade. Other Mock-Oranges can take light shade, but they sacrifice blossoms and grow woodier; must be pruned more often.

Ptelea trifoliata — Hop-Tree. Shrubby, small tree. Must have shade and alkaline or neutral soil. Dark green leaves, aromatic. Bees love the blossoms, which are followed by decorative bunches of round seeds.

Rhamnus — Buckthorn. Vigorous. Handsome foliage and fruits. Good to fill in under trees, or for large hedge. Stands shade.

Rhododendron — See Azalea.

Rhodotypos scandens (R. kerrioides) — Jetbead. Spreading shrub to 6'. Hardy to New England. Clean, bright green foliage conspicuous into autumn. Large, white, four-petaled flowers. Shiny black fruits.

Rhus — *Sumac.* Number of native species good for steep banks partially shaded. Poor, dry soil. Most of them attractive, with handsome pinnate foliage, brilliant red in fall. Flowers good for dried arrangements. *R. canadensis (aromatica)* — Fragrant Sumac. To 3'. 3-part leaves.

Ribes odoratum — Clove Currant. Attractive, old-fashioned shrub to 6'. Tubular, yellow flowers in early spring. Fragrant. Branches good for arranging. Light shade.

Robinia hispida — Rose Acacia. Clusters of pea blossoms of a beautiful rose color make this small awkward shrubby tree an asset. Must be kept within bounds as it seeds prolifically and sends out stolons. Excellent for poor sandy soil where nothing will grow.

Rubus odoratus — Flowering Raspberry. Shreddy canes reaching to 6'. Large, rose-purple flowers. Light red fruit. Bold, maple-like, almost exotic leaves. Likes moist, rich woods, but grows almost anywhere.

Sambucus canadensis — American Elder. Native, rather coarse shrub to 12'. Good for bold effects at woodland borders or in swampy places. Large flat clusters of creamy blossoms, followed by numerous blue-black berries. Handsome from a distance.

Sorbaria sorbifolia — False-Spirea. To 6'. Handsome pinnate leaves like those of the Mountain Ash. Large plumes of creamy white blossoms in summer. Not particular as to soil. Likes shade. Hardy.

Spirea Vanhouttei — To 6′. Gracefully arching branches of rather delicate foliage. Blossoms, profuse, white. Thrives in, and produces blooms in quite heavy shade, but must have good air-circulation. Grows in almost any kind of soil. Thoroughly satisfactory, but not an outstanding shrub. *S. tomentosa* — Steeplebush. Pretty rosy flowers. Native variety. Good for woodland edges. Other spireas will grow in light and partial shade.

Symphoricarpos albus — Snowberry. To 6′. Valued for its large white fruit in autumn. Takes an almost dense shade and is indifferent to soil. *S. orbiculatus* — Indian Currant. With purplish red fruits.

Vaccinium corymbosum — Highbush Blueberry. To 12′, but can be pruned lower. One of best shrubs for acid soil. Lovely creamy white flowers, followed by large blue fruits. Beautiful fall coloring. Must have acid soil, plenty of humus. Use as a landscape shrub; the berries are dividends.

Viburnum. Watch catalogues for Viburnums to best fit your needs. Most will take a light shade. *V. Burkwoodii* is advertised for "sunless places and smoky towns." Some are scraggly, best for woodlands; others make good specimens in the shrub border under tall trees. Some have beautiful white blossoms; others are valued for their brilliant fruits; some have both. Not particular as to soil.

Xanthorhiza simplicissima — Yellow-Root. 2′. Tall groundcover or to dress up shady places. Sharply cut foliage. Drooping racemes of brown-purple flowers in early spring. Grows easily in damp and shade.

Zanthoxylum americanum — Prickly-Ash. To 25′. Usually small prickly shrub. Decorative foilage. White or greenish flowers, followed by black pods with shining black seeds.

Zenobia pulverulenta. Partly evergreen; shrub to 6′. Handsome foliage, gray to gray-green. Flowers; nodding pedicels, white, bell-shaped. Autumn color lovely. Fairly hardy. Sandy acid soil.

11

Evergreen Shrubs

❧✳❧❀❧✳❧❀❧✳❧❀❧✳❧❀❧✳❧❀❧✳❧❀❧✳❧❀❧✳❧❀❧✳❧❀❧✳❧❀❧✳❧❀❧✳❧❀❧✳❧❀❧✳❧❀

EVERGREEN TREES AND SHRUBS form the skeleton of your garden planting. They are the accents in your yard which point up your design. In summer their sturdy greenness serves as a foil for the lighter greens of deciduous trees and shrubs. They make a substantial background for perennials and annuals. In winter they dress up your yard and take away that barren look.

Forms and evergreen colors lend distinction to nude deciduous branches. With evergreens as a background, or as an eye-catcher, you notice for perhaps the first time the bright green of *Kerria* branches. Are we unaware of the outlines of a Beech tree in winter? Let our eye be caught by an evergreen as its neighbor, and at once we are cognizant of the smooth gray Beech bark and the flowing branches tapering to long pointed buds. The low spreading growth of Yews and Junipers dress up the base of almost any tall standing deciduous shrub or tree.

The coniferous evergreens do not offer startling flower

(S. Eric Burgen)

Evergreens can help hide work areas.

display but they have all-year-round foliage that is beautiful, and ideal for flower arrangements. Umbrella-Pine *(Sciadopitys verticillata)* develops artistic curves when planted in light shade. It is lovely in summer as a background for flowers or in front of an upright column of a terrace or porch. Pine boughs are bursts of graceful needles along the branches when brought in with driftwood as a mantelpiece decoration or gracing their parent tree in the open.

Some evergreens have ornamental fruits. The fat cone of a Southern Pine makes a wonderful candlestick holder. The long cones of the Northern White Pine, embellished with their natural white pitch, are often used on branches as winter house-decorations. The small round cones of the Australian Pine *(Casuarina equisetrifolia)* planted in the West and South as windbreaks to hold back sandy soil, can be used in Christmas corsages, as can delicate Hemlock cones.

Holly berries are renowned for use at Christmas time, but have you ever enjoyed a Juniper branch laden with the gray-blue berries? Or the nubbly blue fruits of the *Chamaecyparis?* Bright red berries of Yew with the short dark green needles form a gay Christmas combination in late summer.

Flowering broad-leafed evergreens are spectacular in their blooming periods. A glossy-leafed Magnolia tree studded with white blossom-cups is a picture of stately magnificence. One marvels at the huge mounds of Rhododendrons in the Carolina Mountains. New Hampshire and Massachusetts forests are carpeted with Laurel, making great tangled undergrowths, as Rhododendrons, Salal *(Gaultheria shallon),* and Ferns do in forests in the state of Washington.

In the home garden one small *Andromeda (Pieris floribunda)* with white buds whipping about in late winter winds is a thrilling sign of spring. Bronze *Leucothoe* branches are a picture through fall and winter, emphasized in spring by the delicate reddish tones of the new growth. Croton *(Codiaeum)* with its bright foliage serves to keep the southern garden colorful during sparse blooming periods.

In choosing an evergreen for your garden — as in choosing deciduous material — think of the soil conditions it needs, light, and other requisites. If a shrub grows naturally in shaded or protected areas, place it in similar surroundings in your yard. If swamp-land and wet-feet are what a plant enjoys, do not set it on a dry hillside. This does not mean that such a plant will not grow under ordinary garden conditions, but it will need soil that is well composted and full of humus so that it retains moisture. It will need to be mulched and watered during dry spells. Try to duplicate as nearly as possible a plant's native habitat.

If you have your yard landscaped, get a reliable firm to do it, and make sure that the proper plant material is used for your soil conditions. If you buy the material and do the planting yourself, do a little research beforehand. Know the kinds of plants that your soil will grow best.

If a plant needs what is known as "an acid soil," which all ericaceous plants (Rhododendrons, Laurel, *Leucothoe,* Blueberry, Heather, Wintergreen, Andromeda, Trailing Arbutus, etc.,) must have, it is almost useless to expect it to be healthy in an alkaline or even a neutral soil. Soil must have a pH reading of from about 4.5 to 6.5 to sustain most of the members of the Heath Family. Under natural growths of Oaks and evergreens, the soil is usually at least moderately acid. If you want to know more accurately about your own soil have it tested at a Field Station or test it yourself with litmus paper.

Next to the consideration of soil conditions is your purpose in choosing a shrub for your yard. Do you want it for
bloom? For color in winter? For the birds? For its height?
Bushiness? To fill in a barespot under trees?

If it is for protection from the neighbors or privacy,

(Paul E. Genereux)

Mountain Laurel with Variegated Mint as a ground-cover.

don't try to fill in a large space with a slow-growing type of Yew or a dwarf variety of anything. On the other hand, if you buy a shrub that will eventually become a tree like Arborvitae or that spreads its branches at the top like Witch-Hazel determine whether it will fit the space alloted to it. Native Pines planted on either side of your front steps will soon overshadow your entrance, but Mugho Pines are slow growing, and are attractive additions to the foundation plantings. They have a neat compact form for the most part and although they like sun they will tolerate light shade for a few hours a day.

A yard or even a modest foundation planting can be attractive through all seasons of the year, and it is quite as important to have plant material that appeals to the eye in the fall and winter as it is in the spring. The gray-green of Irish Juniper is often more softly contrasting to brick than the greener green of other plants. All through the winter months, the branches of mountain Andromeda add charm in the form of prominent flower buds.

Contrasting foliages are as important as contrasting outlines of plant materials. A Holly tree next to an Arborvitae is of much greater interest than two Arborvitaes side by side, unless there is the necessity of carrying out a particular planting theme. A tall Pine is more attractive with Rhododendrons at its feet than with other smaller Pines. *Podocarpus* leaves make a better foil for glossy Gardenias and Camellias than the leathery *Pittisporum*.

More things are to be considered in dressing up the outside of your house than in decorating the interior, because plants are always changing. Decorations indoors "stay put" except as you change them. Out of doors they grow and change with each season. You have to see that slow-growing materials are placed where you want plants to remain more or less the same, and use fast-growing plants where you want quick shelter and protection.

It is all very well to turn over your plans to a nursery, but often you will be disappointed. You find out too late that certain plants are not doing well because they have been planted in the wrong place, or too much plant material has been used, or that too many different kinds of shrubs have been crowded into a small area so that there is confusion instead of harmony.

The more you can know about the types of plant materials, the better.

Particular care should be practiced in the moving and planting of evergreens. Their leaves, being evergreen, are continually giving off moisture while the plant is not always able to absorb enough through its roots to counteract what is transpired. This is particularly true in cold weather when the ground is frozen or the soil too cold to allow moisture to be taken up by the root systems.

Any major transplanting of evergreen shrubs or trees can be done safely in early spring just as new growth is about to begin, or in late summer and fall after active growth has stopped, but while there is still time for the shrub to get established before cold weather sets in. Summer, with its heat and aridity, is naturally a poor transplanting season, even though successful moving of plants has been accomplished then. The new idea of spraying leaves with plastic, practiced by some nurseries, helps keep the leaves from giving off excessive moisture.

An evergreen bought at a nursery should have its roots

well balled and burlapped (B & B). Through root-pruning the roots should have been kept in a compact ball, thus enabling the shrub to be moved with little or no disturbance at planting time. In transplanting an evergreen in your yard, or from the wild, where roots have gone their own way in the soil, prepare the new home first and move the shrub quickly with as much earth as possible and with the least possible disturbance of roots and fine root hairs. They resent being torn from their surroundings, and must take time to replenish themselves and reestablish the shrub before it can start to grow.

Even in moving evergreens in the garden, it is well to root-prune them several months in advance. Cut the roots with a sharp spade 6–12″ or more from the main stem (depending on the size of the shrub), completely encircling it while the shrub remains in the ground. In the ensuing months the undisturbed roots will form new roots in a compact mass so the shrub can be moved more easily.

"For a $1.00 plant, dig a $10 hole," is advice well-worth listening to, especially if your soil is as poor as it is around most suburban and city homes. Dig your $10 hole several inches deeper and wider than the plant roots require. Never crowd roots into a hole too small. At the bottom of the hole mix in several spadefuls of rotted compost and leafmold. Mix it thoroughly with the soil or hardpan that is already there. Water the mixture down and add several inches of the best soil available in which to plant your shrub.

If, for any reason, roots seem dry at the time of transplanting, soak them well in water, or water and mud, or see that they are well watered as the shrub is installed. Then set it at its own approximate level. Cut off burlap (if any) to loosen and spread out roots. Around the outside edges of the roots, place more good soil so that the fine-root hairs can push out easily as they grow. In the space between the roots and the outside edge of the hole, replace some of the poor soil mixed with compost. Set the shrub as you want it, tamp earth firmly around it, water it well so that the soil can settle about the roots and not leave air pockets. Continue filling up available space with compost, or compost mixed with soil, leaving a slight depression at the top to catch and hold excess water. Through the coming season keep it well-watered during dry spells, seeing that the evergreen needles or leaves are watered occasionally too to compensate for transpiration.

In transplanting evergreens — or any shrubs — the first job of the gardener is to encourage the growth of strong roots, even at sacrifice of flowers the first year. Cut off buds and blossoms to send the plant's strength down toward the roots. Evergreens do not usually require severe branch pruning, although where many roots have been mutilated in transplanting, it might be necessary to cut off top or side branches in order to compensate. After that prune only to keep plant in shape, a branch here and there that grows beyond the limits of a formal "cone" or "ball," or an ungainly side growth that detracts from the artistic outlines.

Evergreens with fine-needled foliage or scale-like foliage should be kept sheared to encourage their natural shape, but not so severely that they look artificial — unless of course the owner likes the look of formality. Late spring or early summer is the best time for this light shearing. Broad-leaved evergreens seldom need anything but a dead or dying branch cut off here and there, or a light pruning to shape. For decorations and flower arrangements, however, branches of any evergreens can be cut any time of the year (although too severe winter cutting is never good). In cutting for use, choose

Branches of evergreens, like the Box here, can be
cut any time of year for flower arrangements.

branches that are both artistic and that the shrub will not miss. Cut them carefully back to the joint of another branch. Never leave stubs showing. Be discriminating in the cutting of your slow-growing evergreens such as the Umbrella Pine, Laurel, Andromeda, but part of your fun in growing them is to enjoy them. If that enjoyment be for indoors, learn to prune them wisely and carefully.

LIST OF EVERGREEN SHRUBS THAT TOLERATE SHADE

Araucaria auracana — Monkey-Puzzle Tree, so named because the sharp-pointed, overlapping needles make it a puzzle for even a monkey. Interesting. Not hardy in the North. *A. excelsa* — Norfolk-Island-Pine. Similar. Neither likes crowding or burning sunlight. Both can be used as house plants.

Arbutus unedo — Strawberry-Tree. Conspicuous and interesting for its red bark. Not hardy in North. A shrub in many places; small tree in warm climates. Drooping clusters of white or pinkish flowers in fall, together with ripe, strawberry-like fruits from previous years' flowers. Acid soil.

Aucuba japonica — 4–5′. Dark, lustrous foliage. Need both sexes for decorative red berries. Moist, fertile soil, but withstands shade, smoky conditions, some sea air. Hardy to Washington. Variegated variety called Gold-dust-tree.

Azara microphylla — Handsome shrub 8–12′. Flat sprays of small glittering leaves. Tiny yellow flowers in February, inconspicuous but highly fragrant. Likes humidity, some shade. Hardy to Washington.

Berberis Sargentiana — Sargent Barberry. To 6′. Handsome, with dark green leaves. Reddish branches when young. Hardy. *B. Darwinii* — Darwin's Barberry. Dark, glistening Holly-like leaves. Drooping clusters orange-yellow flowers in spring. Berries purplish blue. Some shade and moist, fertile soil. Not hardy. Numerous other varieties.

Buxus sempervirens — Box. 3–25′. Shrubby. Neat, tidy, of slow growth. Small dark leaves. Background or filler-plant: makes good hedges; good for cutting. Choice.

Camellia. Naturally shapely shrubs; good for background planting. Small shrubs can be fillers. Slow growers. Valued for ornamental properties and the white, pink, red, and variegated blossoms through winter. Will stand some frost, but prefer a moderate climate with high humidity. Acid soil, shade, compost, and old manure.

Chamaecyparis — False-Cypress. Attractive, feathery-foliaged evergreen much used for foundation planting. *C. obtusa* and *C. pisifera* and many varieties are good. Numerous sizes, shapes, and colors. Consult local nurseries. Likes moisture, humus, partial shade, and plenty of air.

Daphne odora — Sweet Daphne. 2–3′. Leathery, glossy foliage. Waxy, fragrant, white-purple flowers. Difficult. Probably acid soil.

Fatsia japonica. Glossy, deeply-lobed leaves. Long panicles of white flowers. Tropical effect. Easy to grow. Hardy to New Jersey. *Fatshedera* — "Miracle plant." A cross between *Fatsia* and *Hedera*. Lovely, glossy, pointed leaves, good for arranging.

Gardenia jasminoides. To 6′. Beautiful, glossy dark leaves. Creamy white, fragrant flowers. Not hardy, but grown indoors in the North. Acid soil, fibrous loam (rough compost) with old manure. Likes humidity, some sun in winter (indoors), shade from hot sun in summer.

Gaultheria Shallon — Salal. Native to West, but hardy in other places to lower Massachusetts. Leathery, dark green leaves, heart-shaped. Panicles of pinky white flowers. Grows straight and sturdy under trees; sprawls in the sun. Should be used more.

Hamelia patens. 5–15′. Subtropical, but can be grown in greenhouses. Blooms for months — bright orange-red tubular blossoms. Leaves sometimes red or purplish. If struck down by frost, blooms the following summer.

Ilex opaca — Holly. Glossy, spiny, dark green leaves. Red berries. Two sexes needed for berries. Rich soil, acid; partial shade. *I. aquifolium* — English Holly. *I. crenata* and varieties —Glossy leaves; like Boxwood. *I. glabra* — Inkberry. Hardy, native shrub. Black berries. Other good species. Many varieties.

Illicium floridanum — Anise-Tree. Tender evergreen with elliptic aromatic leaves. Dark red flowers. Acid soil. Partial shade.

Juniperus chinensis Pfitzeriana — Pfitzer Juniper. Branches dense, blue-green plumes. Beautiful. Low, spreading. Good for difficult banks. Although the Junipers are sun-loving and will stand heat and wind, a few will stand some shade — *J. communis* and *J. horizontalis plumosa*.

Kalmia latifolia — Mountain-Laurel. One of the most beautiful shrubs for northern gardens. Slow-growing. Leaves glossy, dark green. Showy flowers in terminal clusters, white to deep pink. Good for foundation planting or bankings. Likes humus and moisture, but will stand aridity if well-mulched. Acid soil. Pruned easily to shape.

Laurus nobilis — Laurel. Sweet Bay. To 50′, but shrubby when young. The Laurel of poetry and romance. Requirements similar to its northern counterpart. Not hardy. Leathery aromatic leaves. Greenish yellow flowers followed by black berries. A good hedge plant; stands hard pruning.

Leiophyllum — Sand-Myrtle. To 18″. Small, lustrous evergreen leaves. Waxy white blossoms, similar to those of Blueberries. Useful for rock gardens and to border evergreen plantings. Sandy acid soil. Can stand partial shade.

Leucothoe Catesbaei. To 6′. Handsome broad-leafed evergreen. Arching branches, turn lustrous bronze in fall. Lovely pink and bronze new growth. Flower-arranger's dream. Nodding white flowers. Compost, acid soil. Shade and protection from wind.

Ligustrum — Privet. Many species and varieties; each has its place. Some, half-evergreen. Foliage, neat and lustrous. Flowers, white in small or large clusters. Grows almost anywhere; endures almost anything. Few pests or diseases. Not particular as to soil. Most will stand a good deal of shade, many growing to young trees in northern city-gardens. Many known as hedge plants. Near a garden, the roots like to "walk."

Lycium sinense — Chinese Wolfberry. Half-evergreen. Arching branches to 10′. Spiny. Profusion of small purple flowers; showy display of orange-red berries. *L. halimifolium* — Matrimony-Vine. Smaller flowers and fruits. Good for shady corner where it can take over. Suckers freely.

Mahonia aquifolium — Oregon Grape. 3–5′. Handsome, dark green spiny leaves like Holly leaves. Golden flowers; blue berries. Hardy to Boston. Tolerates many conditions. Leaves sometimes winter-kill in winds, but the new foliage soon makes the shrub beautiful again. Other species and several varieties.

Michelia fuscata — Banana-Shrub. To 15′. Popular evergreen of the South. Shiny leaves. Yellow and purple flowers in the axils; banana-like fragrance. Humus and partial shade.

Nandina domestica — Heavenly Bamboo. 6–8′. Considered tender but has survived near New York. Neatly constructed shrub. Fern-like leaves, tinted copper when new. White flowers in summer. Bright red berries. Likes leafmold and moisture.

Osmanthus illicifolius — Holly Osmanthus. To 20′. Lustrous, evergreen leaves, spiny. Fragrant white flowers. Hardy to New York, possibly Massachusetts. Other species grown in South. Sun or partial shade. Protection in North.

Photinia arbutifolia — Toyon. 15′. Grows best and most in California. Arbutus-like foliage. Large flat heads of white flowers; followed by beautiful red berries. Likes a cool hillside. *P. serrulata.*

Pieris floribunda — Mountain Andromeda. Small, dense evergreen to 6'. Neat. Slow-growing. Good for foundation planting. Nodding white flowers. One of best shrubs. *P. japonica* — Japanese Andromeda. White pendulous blossoms. Lustrous foliage. Reddish and pink new growth in spring is beautiful. Neat; upright manner of growth.

Pinus Mugo Mughus — Mugho Pine. Rounded prostrate shrub with interesting manner of growth. Light shade. Plenty of humus.

Pittosporum Tobira — Japanese Pittosporum. 6–10'. Thick, leathery leaves. Flowers, white or yellowish, fragrant. Tender, but stands various conditions. Good hedge plant.

Raphiolepsis umbellata — Yeddo-Hawthorn. Low-growing. Mild climate. Thick, lustrous leaves. Clusters of fragrant white flowers.

Rhododendron catawbiense. 6–12'. One of best evergreens. Foliage lustrous and not too large. Flowers, prolific and beautiful except for color. Many improved hybrids. Pruned easily to shape. Acid soil; full of rough humus; shade; protected from winds. Hardy to Boston and North. *R. maximum.* Blooms a month or so later, not so beautiful because new growth tends to hide flowers. Hardier than preceding. *R. carolinianum* — Carolina Rhododendron. To 6'. Smaller all around. A favorite. Choose flowers for good pink color. Other Rhododendrons are hardy to Boston, but are not yet well-known.

Ruscus aculeatus — Butcher's Broom. To 4'. Green stems. Leaf-like, flattened branches. Enjoyed for winter berries. Also, branches dried and dyed for indoor use. Withstands heat, sun, shade.

Sarcococca rustifolia — Fragrant Sarcococca. To 6'. Not hardy. Lustrous evergreen foliage. Small, fragrant flowers, white.

Can stand shade and drip of trees. Has lived in New England with protection.

Skimmia. Low attractive shrubs. Withstands city conditions, but not hardy north of Washington, D.C. Fragrant panicles of flowers. Red or black fruits, but needs shrubs of both sexes.

Taxus — Yew. Useful for many purposes. Upright and spreading types with many intermediates. Dark green needles in good condition winter and summer. Grows almost anywhere, in sun or shade. Likes moisture. *T. cuspidata nana* is the accepted name for slow-growing Japanese type. Prune only when needed.

Thuja — Arbor Vitae. To 60′. Slow-growing varieties developed for home use; columns and globular shapes, some with almost yellow foliage. Likes cool climates, however; dislikes heat and aridity.

Tsuga canadensis — Canadian Hemlock. Graceful, attractive evergreen with needle-like, almost feathery foliage. A tree, it can be pruned to shrub proportions for many years. Likes humus and moisture.

Part Three

Planning and Maintaining the Shady Garden

12

Something About Design

⤝✳⥤❂⤝✳⥤❂⤝✳⥤❂⤝✳⥤❂⤝✳⥤❂⤝✳⥤❂⤝✳ ❂⤝✳⥤❂⤝✳⥤❂⤝✳⥤❂⤝✳⥤❂⤝✳⥤❂⤝✳⥤❂

MANY PEOPLE ARE AFRAID of design in a garden, thinking it is for the wealthy or the very artistic and not for the person who merely wants to enjoy a few trees and flowers. They may think they want natural plantings, as nature would have them, little realizing that the most successful natural gardens have been created through good design. In fact, the most successful gardens of any kind are those which have been planned with considerable thought and a feeling of artistic creation, if not a careful layout on paper.

The smallest house and garden, well-arranged and decorated, can be a gem of artistic merit. A fortune does not have to be spent on it, or a wealth of material used. The gardener does not have to be a recognized artist even though (consciously or unconsciously) he follows certain rules of design.

Many of these rules can be classed as plain common sense. Something looks right, or it doesn't look right. No one would knowingly plant a tall perennial in front of a low-growing shrubby plant. It is common sense to arrange plants so that they can be seen to advantage — tall perennials in back of low perennials, a conical-shaped tree in the center of a group of evergreen shrubs rather than at the outside. It is common sense to have accent plants here and there, to stress a corner, or point up entrances to attract the eye in some way. Otherwise, a planting lacks character. It is common sense to have a theme to your planting, which consists of plants similar in size, shape, or other characteristic to create unity and harmony. Too many different kinds of plants result in confusion.

We are most apt to find shaded areas around large old houses, and in a way they are the most difficult to fit into the landscape. Many of these houses are too high for their width, or they are architecturally bad, or they are too close to the street, which accentuates their height. Shrubs and trees can either call attention to these architectural defects, or be so cleverly arranged that we think of the picture as an attractive whole and not as a group of faulty details.

If a house seems too high, a good-sized evergreen of conical shape such as Hemlock, Fir, or Spruce placed 6–10 feet from a front corner of the house will "step the house down" so that it looks wider. A large deciduous tree (Linden, Maple, Jacaranda), or a group of large shrubs away from the house, should be situated so that they break the upright line of the house. Tall established trees near the street, or property lines, tend to set a house in scale and give it a look of permanence.

Large bushes and shrubs should be used around large houses. Large-leaved Ivy and Rhododendrons with large leaves are usually better suited to planting around the foundation of a large house than Andromedas and Laurel, though these can be worked in with other plants so that the planting is on a large scale even though individual plants may be small. In the South, *Monstera deliciosa* climbing the trunk of a tree

This stepping-stone path leads to a picnic table; the line of the shrubbery planting follows it.

would be in good proportion to a large building. If your house is large and you want a dwarf Alberta Spruce with fine delicate needles, place it in a small area rather than setting it near the house where its delicate features would be lost.

A few years ago most houses, if they were landscaped at all, were be-fronted with mounded evergreens like rows of fat pigeons. These were usually needled varieties — Chamaecyparis, Cypress, Yews, Arborvitaes, ect. — clipped and manicured with neat precision. Often the shrubs completely surrounded a house, setting it in sort of a frame. This foundation planting was supposed to hide the foundation and enhance the dwelling.

Today, with our tendency toward simpler living, comes simpler planting. People prefer fewer shrubs but those few set in spots that matter. Owners give more thought to type of shrub, variety, and manner of growth. They consider the reason for each tree and shrub, the purpose it serves, and any additional use.

The purpose of any foundation planting is still to make the house more attractive. It can also hide some of the foundation, but many foundations are not unattractive. If there is a bad feature, hide it by all means, but don't hide everything. A brick chimney is far more appealing with Ivy creeping up at random than with its lower portion completely smothered in overgrown evergreens.

Foundation planting requires as much thought as any major indoor project. What do you want to accomplish in planting the outside of your home? You want to make it attractive and interesting. Do you want a variety of shrubs, an attractive combination of both needled and broad-leafed evergreens, plus a few deciduous shrubs for spring gayety? If you are a flower arranger, you must have shrubs to cut for indoor use. If you have children, you should choose shrubs to withstand their feet and bicycles. Perhaps you want shrubs easily cared for, or you may be willing to spend a little time on them and include a few distinctive ones. Plant material must enhance the house, but must also satisfy your personal requirements.

The front door, usually the most important part of a house, is the first place to consider; here is where you welcome your friends. If the front door is attractive, the planting can be simple — an interesting shrub at either side to play up its beauty. If it is an ordinary one, dress it up with a more elaborate planting. If it has definitely ugly features, either hide them or play them down so that the visitor is not aware of them. Unusual and distinctive shrubs are needed here — evergreens chosen for form or interesting foliage or a rare, small tree with good seasonal interest. Place them so that they will barely touch each other when full maturity is reached.

Perhaps your side door is the one you and your friends use most of the time. Then you'll probably want to settle for a simple, formal front-door planting and dress up your side door with vines or other intimate plantings. Back doors need attention, depending on space and exposure. Complete informality can take over there, even to a garbage can set in a bed of Lilies-of-the-Valley.

Before doing any landscaping, study your house and yard from all angles, inside and out. Which features do you want to obliterate, and which do you want to play up? Perhaps a porch or terrace should be sheltered or protected, or you have a special window from which you'd like to see a flowering tree or other feature. And would the planting look attractive from the front of the house? From the side?

Consider whether your house is formal or informal, and

try to suit the planting to the architecture as well as to the layout of the land. A city house has less land and suggests more formal planting than one in the country. A suburban house can be formal or informal, according to architecture and neighborhood. In the country or in small towns, houses usually have a country flavor about them; those of more or less formal design can stand informal plantings because of the very nature of their location.

Various types of houses call for special landscaping. A Cape Cod cottage suggests climbing roses whereas a three-storied stone dwelling might call for Ivy and unclipped evergreens. A formal tapestry brick house needs broad-leaved evergreens well combined with needled evergreens. A stucco house in the deep South would seem lost without a palm of some sort. The extremely modern house might call for a "Trylon and Perisphere" planting carried out with conical Fir and rounded *Taxus,* or some other planting along modern lines.

Plant material should conform to your ideas; if a triangle of three different-sized Cedars is needed at the side of a high house to "step it down," three palm trees would not create the same effect. Neither would three cedars all the same height.

If you planted *Daphne Merzereum* at a corner of a small box-like house the shrub would actually do nothing for it, but a rampant Forsythia or large, shrubby Azalea immediately makes the house seem wider. Its limiting lines are softened by the various and indefinite lines of the shrub. An evergreen of formal columnar outline would follow too closely the upright lines of the house and "chop it off."

For a modern ranch-style house with long, low lines, a half dozen Arbor Vitae set every 6–8 feet across the front would do nothing to carry out the long low line; they would break the very rhythm the architect had tried to create. Follow those house lines with a low hedge or series of plants of the same height and type.

Your question becomes not merely WHAT to plant and WHERE, but "How shall I make my house look as if it belonged to its plot of land?" Every house cannot look as if it "grew," but any house or building can be enhanced if thought is given to the landscaping around it. Even if the planting is unorthodox, if it seems right for your house and you, then it *is* right. But don't go into it blindly. You won't know what you want until you know what is available and how it can be used to serve your purpose. Read articles; study books on landscaping and design; consult local garden groups and horticultural societies.

A house built with the contour of an uneven plot of land should have planting that adheres to the topography. Consider a steep bank somewhere near the home. If planted with shrubs and vines, along winding brick or stone steps, it will be far more attractive than planted to deciduous trees with gaunt, bare trunks. An unattractive slope at the side of a house can be made into a beautiful terrace with a stone wall. Even a path downhill to a picnic area, or clothesyard, planted with the right material, becomes an invitation rather than an eyesore.

A house in the middle of a flat plot of land is at once more formal, less interesting. Not so much imagination is needed to make it into an acceptable home, but more is needed to make it into an unusual home. Areas must be divided according to needs, yet not obviously, and so that each area leads into the next and one feels an urge to progress about the yard. In small places this is not easy, yet it is surprising what can be done by strategic planting of shrubs and trees.

For a look of settled living around a new home, use a few good-sized shrubs rather than a number of small ones. True, the small ones will grow, but if you desire a yard demanding little care, choose slow-growing shrubs that need little pruning, plant them well and keep them mulched with peat moss or a ground cover. Do not use trees as shrubs, unless you are aware that you'll have to dig them up or cut them down in about ten years.

The planting close to the house serves to make the building more attractive and ties it to the ground, but the yard planting should tie the house to the general landscape, whether it be woods, open country, or neighboring yards. Consequently this planting should be in keeping with the general landscape. An exotic house in the North surrounded by tropical plants with strange leaves, would seem out of place with Cape Cod cottages in a New England village, even if they would endure the cold.

In like manner, a Cape Cod house on one of the Florida Keys, with planting typically New England, would not be at home among palm trees and Spanish moss. True, people have built homes that are different, which are acceptable and even effective, but when a house is one of a row typical of the locality, and differs radically from its neighbors, it becomes too conspicuous for good taste. Keep your house and yard in character with the neighborhood unless you are isolated and can afford to do as you please.

Due to the nature of our subject, we are considering here mostly yards with established trees, and lucky is he who has them to consider. By their very nature, they help both house and yard to fit into the surrounding territory, and can enhance a beautiful house or make an ugly one more attractive. They give shade in summer and raise the temperature in winter. They add beauty of form and foliage to summer enjoyment (to say nothing of flowers and berries) and give interest to the winter scene. They can lend privacy to a yard; and shut out noise and confusion of traffic. They help act as a watershed, their leaves breaking the fall of hard rains and their roots forming a natural sponge that serves as a reservoir for surplus water. Their branches are good for cutting. Against a spring sky, their unfolding buds make patterns unsurpassed by any of man's designs. They are refuges for birds which we need in our yards to help combat insects. They offer all kinds of possibilities to children. And they bring pleasure to friends within our gates, and to the millions of passers-by who may never know us, but who, on catching a glimpse of the spreading boughs, like us because they like our trees.

Although a few trees in a small yard are beneficial, too many can cause problems. A few give shade; an excess tends to shut out light and air and make a house damp. Though we take leaf-raking in stride, raking up an over-abundance of acorns, horse chestnuts, etc., can be a nuisance. If you "inherit" a number of trees, consider whether all of them are necessary, particularly if shrubs and other plants are trying to grow under them. Some shrubs and perennials will survive the stifling atmosphere of heavy sweeping boughs, but a great many plants will grow and bloom under trees if the lower branches have been removed so that light and air can

(*Gottscho-Schleisner*)

Accessories that are interesting and add to the beauty of the landscape.

filter through the upper ones. Too many trees planted close together, grow spindling; if they have been properly thinned for garden enjoyment, one or two can develop into magnificent specimens that become valuable assets.

Your own personal reasons must guide your planting, or removal, of surplus trees. If you love trees, but desire an attractive yard, you will sacrifice one or two for the benefit of order and design. Your decision might not come immediately for one must live with a house and yard to know it. It takes time to realize which trees should be eliminated and which allowed to stand. Their growing habits, locations, beauty, the shadows they cast are all considerations in building your yard to one of comfortable beauty.

Yard planting (as compared to foundation planting) becomes one of boundary lines, to insure privacy; of making the yard more interesting; of enhancing and dividing certain areas into play-yard, clothesyard, etc.; of serving as a transition between the yard and the natural environment; and of acting as further link between the house and established trees.

In these various capacities shrubs, and trees used as shrubs, are usually planted in groups or masses in contrast to being considered as individuals near a house. If bold effects are desired, attractive plant-pictures can be enjoyed from a distance; tree trunks are surrounded with low evergreens. A driveway might be emphasized on either side with a tree of definite outline (such as a pointed Spruce) or a large group of shrubs with a tree as a focal point. When traffic must be dulled, and space is at a premium, use a fence, wall, or hedge of narrow evergreens (placed 2–3′ apart) that can be pruned to the space. In greater areas plant an informal shrub-and-tree-border. Evergreens like Hemlocks are admirable for this purpose — a front row, 10–12′ apart, with a second row, about

10′ from the first, and staggered so that the trees in the second row come between the trees in the first row. A more heterogeneous border can be used if desired. Then, tall material like Firs or Spruces should serve as accents in your skyline, with lower growing evergreens or deciduous shrubs planted in front, and between them.

In such a border, plants of delicate texture and form are lost. Bright colors, large leaves, bold forms, and striking outlines are called for.

There are further considerations before a yard can be designed and planted. First, the needs it will have to serve for the kind of family who owns it. If there are young children a play-yard with swings, sandbox, etc., should be included. If there are older children with a liking for strenuous sports space must be allowed. Perhaps the family want a vegetable garden; a cutting garden; or for bird-lovers, special shrubs.

Most people move into a house that is already built, with established driveway, garage, and other features, and a yard more or less divided into various areas. If the general layout is satisfactory, good; but once in a while the new owner has ideas that do not conform to those already established. In that case a change is inevitable. Yet it is usually best to live with a house for a while before doing anything radically different.

Rhythm is one of the important principles of design. The lines in a garden must have direction; they must go somewhere, or they must come back; there must be a reason for their being. In a small yard a long line leads one on and gives greater feeling of space or scale. If the yard is large, a line can become too long, creating a feeling of monotony, and should be broken. The lines of a yard or the planting should follow lines already established (as of house, driveway, edge of property, etc.); or else be diametrically opposed to established lines. But they must be arranged so that there is a definite feeling of rhythm.

(Paul E. Genereux)

The tree breaks the upright lines of the house, and the yard planting ties the house to the landscape.

There must be harmony in plantings just as harmony in the interior of a house. Types and sizes of plant materials should blend to present a unified whole. Harmony is created in part by a predominance of one plant or type of plant. Yet too many plants of one kind, unless used for a specific purpose (hedge, etc.) are monotonous. Strive for a happy medium.

Like colors in a room, subordinated to a dominant hue, manipulate plants, employing the unusual, distinctive, or very different ones sparingly. Used thus, these contrasting materials catch the eye, cause a feeling of interest.

In various plantings consider plant-materials of three types:

1. *Dominant or high accent points*. In large plantings these can be used as a theme. They are plants that stand out in size or shape so that we are immediately struck by them, such as pointed Firs in a shrubbery-and-tree border, or groups of *Digitalis* in a perennial flower bed.

2. *Mass or Filler types* are plants that lend themselves to background planting, that can be used as a theme or as a transition from high accent plants to low plants. Sometimes the mass type of plant can be individually distinctive in form (such as Laurel or types of *Pittisporum*); used together they present a mass against which to plant other materials of contrasting form or color. They let the eye rest, whereas dominant plants catch the attention and hold it.

3. *Interest or low accent type*. Usually low-growing, these are often of definite interest only at certain times. The Christmas-Rose *(Helleborus niger)* and its cousin, *Helleborus orientalis,* are good examples. Their blossoms come during the winter, but in warm weather their evergreen leaves are of enough interest to make good contrast for the mass type of growth surrounding them. Maidenhair-fern, *Hosta,* and

Epimedium can all be used as interest types, framed and backed by plants of intermediate growth.

Whether flower bed or shrubbery border, the planting should have variation in height. Except when used as a hedge or for some definite aspect, plants of the same height are uninteresting when placed together. A pointed Fir gives strength and meaning to a group of low-growing evergreens, just as a single outstanding evergreen accents a group of deciduous trees or shrubs. Have you ever gazed at a flower bed solid with peonies and wondered why it lacked interest? A peony bush is a mass type of plant and needs added height and low accent plants used with it. Place a peony in front of the tall spires of Monkshood and immediately you have a plant-picture with an interesting skyline.

Beware of introducing too many high points. This causes a choppy picture. Use high accents when needed, with good transition from low to high. Make the picture easy for the eye to look upon and to scan.

Have shrub-planting, paths, perennial borders and other garden areas in the right proportion. Paths and walks should be wide enough to be practical. Garden areas around large trees can be larger than those around small trees. If there is space for a long perennial border, 6–8' wide is about right; shorter border-gardens can be narrower. If the perennial bed is against a tall tree boundary border it can be wider than if against a low shrub border or fence. Plants too small around a large house make the house top-heavy; plants too large around a small house look top-heavy themselves.

To be attractive a garden should have good display value. This is particularly true in a shady garden where flowers are fewer and more emphasis is placed on the locations of individual plants. When you set in a bush, tree, or even a peren-

nial, try to determine whether it will look the way you want
it to look from several different locations. Plant flowers so that
they show. Six Tulips growing near a house might be adequate for the space and make a well-proportioned and balanced picture, but if these same six Tulips were planted 100'
from the house and were to be viewed across the 100', they
would be lost.

Use bolder materials and lighter hues in shady gardens.
White, yellow, and pink are good colors. They give life to the
shadows. Plant small flowers in large masses, or use big flowers,
such as King Alfred Daffodils, if they are to be enjoyed from
a distance. Species Tulips and Narcissi, and delicate little wild
flowers, belong in intimate small spaces where they can be
seen from a path, the house, or a terrace.

Average yards are usually broken up into areas; the
front, or "Welcome Area," the back, side, or "Service Area,"
and the "Garden Area." On large estates there will be more
sections, each of which however, fits into one of the above
categories. In small yards two areas might be thrown into one.
Whichever way it is, consider each area a circle or oval with an
imaginary central axis line through the length and width.
The plant materials and other furnishings placed on either
side of the axis line should balance each other, either sym-
metrically or asymmetrically.

Balance in art is the visual weight on either side of an
imaginary central axis. Symmetrical balance occurs when the
two sides are furnished identically — a front door in the center of a house with a grouping of three plants set at identical
spots on either side of it. Symmetrical balance in foundation
planting usually occurs when the house itself is rather formal

in outline, with the front door in the center, and the two walls similar in architecture.

Asymmetrical balance occurs when two sides are planted differently, but arranged with architectural and other features so that the resulting picture looks balanced. A front door placed toward the right end of a house would look over-weighted if too heavily planted. Stretches of windows, bay windows, and other features of the house must be taken into consideration. A bare space in the wall might call for a large broad-leaved evergreen or an espaliered tree, to offset windows or other feature in another wall. The imaginary axis line is drawn through the center of the front wall, from roof to foundation; plantings and architectural embellishments are weighed on both sides.

A formal garden can easily be imagined. Asymmetrically balanced gardens are a little more difficult. An entrance at the right of a garden might balance a large old tree at the back, to the left. And by garden, is meant not merely a space for flowers, but a laid-out design of lawn, terrace, shrubs, trees, flowers, or anything that fits into the general plan. Perhaps the tree is a beautiful gnarled Oak that completely dominates the scene.

In one garden I know an informal winding path begins at a low stone wall and twists through a small, but well-planted perennial bed toward the Oak, which is a focal point for the entire area. As the tree is a little to the left of the imaginary axis-line, there is an evergreen shelter belt at the right, between yard and street, which serves to give the garden balance. It seems a simple design. One is not aware of any rules being followed, but the rules are there, and the result is a charming, inviting natural garden-path which offers relaxation and peace.

In planning a path or driveway, it is well to make it as straight as possible without sacrificing looks. A curve in a walk or path is graceful only if necessary and right. Eliminate odd angles and twists.

A backyard area that serves as a clothesyard and service area can also include a children's play-yard. Perhaps a picnic space can be included with a modest fireplace. Make it low by piling field-stones in a semi-circle, larger ones on the bottom. It will be just as satisfactory and more artistic than an expensive, cemented "mausoleum."

In furnishing the outdoor living rooms, choose accessories that are interesting and definitely add to the beauty — or service — of the landscape. Remember color schemes. A red sand box is a vivid spot on the landscape, but a purple Magnolia planted near it . . . ? Orange trapezes are gay, but pink Roses climbing on nearby trellises are snubbed with the ostentation of the brighter color. Choose with restraint your little white ducks, flamingoes, chickens, mushrooms, dwarfs. One or two might be all right, but gardens as well as houses should be furnished in good taste. Spend your money on plants!

13

Special Gardens

⤚❊⤙◉⤚❊⤙◉⤚❊⤙◉⤚❊⤙◉⤚❊⤙◉⤚❊⤙◉⤚❊⤙◉⤚❊⤙◉⤚❊⤙◉⤚❊⤙◉⤚❊⤙◉⤚❊⤙◉⤚❊⤙◉

THE CITY GARDEN

MOST CITY GARDENS are small, consisting usually of a rectangle of poor earth at the back of the house, or sometimes an additional pocket-handkerchief of a front yard. Space is at a premium. If a real garden is desired, plant materials which make the most of the space, must be chosen; two-dimension plants which go up and to the side, but not out in front; or whose branches can be kept pruned that way.

Occasionally a tiny path can be introduced from the back-door to the lower left-hand corner, say, across the lot to the opposite corner, cutting the yard into two triangles, but planted so that the whole is in balance. Perhaps there is a tree near the back-door. With furniture grouped around it, on a wide brick walk or terrace, its shadows offer cool respite from which to view a quiet border garden. Even a tiny pool can be introduced. Plant evergreens and bulbs around it. Use brick walks to set off the design.

In city gardens the shade cast by buildings as well as by trees must be taken into consideration. On fairly wide streets plants on either side usually receive 4–6 hours of sun a day and shade the rest of the time. At least in one large eastern city, Magnolias stand this condition very successfully. They bloom earlier than their suburban counterparts, and spring shoppers look for the magnificent blossoms as eagerly as the city dwellers.

(Paul E. Genereux)

A city garden planted to vines and potted plants.

Much has been said about plants enduring dust, smoke, and smog of cities. They don't like them, it is true, particularly broad-leaved evergreens whose pores get clogged; but in most instances, poor growth of plants is blamed on city conditions more than on lack of organic material in the soil. In many city gardens the evergreens would not have to struggle so hard if the soil were turned over once in a while and had incorporated in it some of the leaves that are annually raked up and burned.

It's odd how some people expect their plants to thrive in any kind of soil. City people will tell you how hard it is to buy manure, but there are leaves on city trees and weeds that could be rescued from vacant lots. These organic materials — like anything that once grew in the soil — can be turned back into it.

One compost pile in a city garden is as small as you'd ever hope to see, wedged between the back of a building and the edge of the property. Very few trees grow in this vicinity so that the owner has to visit trees several blocks away before the street department gets there with rakes and matches. He also keeps his eye "peeled" for certain weeds in neglected city lots, and knows the spots where people dump their meager grass clippings. He piles all these together, with egg shells, coffee grounds, pea pods, etc. Boards hold them down and preserve moisture and a little ground limestone keeps flies away and obliterates odors. After a year or so, this compost dug into the soil, accomplishes miracles. There are roses in the tiny garden. There are Chrysanthemums, a Cardinal Climber, Tomato plants, *Hosta,* and a few bulbs. This forgotten spot jammed in between alley and buildings has been turned into a lovely garden.

Many plants will not grow in a city. Besides poor soil

(Paul E. Genereux)

One of the famous Beacon Hill gardens in the heart of Boston.

there is not always enough air-circulation. Coal dust and oil fumes are too much for some of the fussier plants. Try shade-enduring ones that grow easily. Give them the best possible conditions, as much compost and peat moss as possible, good cultivating and mulching. Plants as well as people respond to the right treatment.

TREES IN A CITY

Trees in a city, as well as being able to withstand shade, must be drought-resistant. Not only must they endure a natural lack of rain and other watering, but their roots often have to seek far for available nutrients in the soil made possible by rain seeping through a few cracks of a city street or sidewalk. A few trees that endure the conditions we impose upon them are:

Acer platanoides — Norway Maple. Tolerant of smoke, dust, shade. Tougher than, but similar in size and shape to the Sugar Maple, *A. saccharum.* Used extensively but should have room to spread. One of America's most beautiful trees.

Ailanthus altissima — Tree of Heaven. Attractive.

Aralia spinosa — Devil's-Walking-Stick. Grows anywhere. Seeds itself anywhere.

Carpinus — Hornbeam. Hardy. Slow-growing. Stands pruning.

Ginkgo biloba. (Male type) Upright growth. Extremely tolerant. Interesting; fan-shaped leaves.

Ostrya virginiana — Hop-Hornbeam. Similar to Hornbeam. Both excellent, but little known. Withstands dryness. Attractive.

Phellodendron— Cork-Tree. Hardy. Adaptable, but needs room to spread. Attractive; aromatic foliage.

A spot between buildings and an alley transformed into a pleasant garden.

Platanus acerifolia — London Plane-Tree. Used extensively as street tree. Endures pruning. Hardy to Massachusetts. *P. occidentalis* — Buttonwood. Native variety. Good.

Prunus serotina — Black Cherry. Lumber tree, exceedingly tolerant of city conditions. Edible fruit.

Sophora japonica — Chinese Scholar-Tree. Slow-growing, but eventually large. Blooms in summer. Hardy to Boston.

Tilia americana — American Linden. Large beautiful tree, not used enough. *T. vulgaris* — European Linden. Smaller; pyramidal; beautiful.

Tsuga canadensis — Hemlock. Given a good start in compost, makes an excellent city-yard tree. Beautiful. Graceful.

SHRUBS IN A CITY

Yews *(Taxus)* will stand almost anything and are used extensively for city plantings. They thrive if the soil is improved by compost and leafmold, but they'll struggle along where the soil is poor and eroded. If upright evergreens are desired, try *Thuya,* the variety that stays green all winter. Humus in the soil retains the moisture it loves. In yard plantings Pines and Hemlocks can be used as shrubs. They grow slowly in a city, but well-planted they usually prove satisfactory.

The same can be said about the broad-leaved evergreens: Laurel, Andromeda, Holly, *Mahonia*, Rhododendrons. They like to have their leaves washed once in awhile.

Flowering shrubs, if they'll stand any shade at all, grow better in a city than evergreens because their leaves renew themselves each spring and have to combat the dust only during the summer. Redbuds and Dogwoods flourish under the right city conditions. Azaleas in gorgeous array fill city parks. Forsythia endures almost anything, and what a joy it is on a city street banking instead of straggly grass.

Flowering Quince does beautifully under city conditions, as does the Smoke-Tree *(Cotinus coggygria)*. The Siberian Pea-Tree *(Caragana arborescens)*, with silvery gray foliage an excellent contrast to the darker shades of evergreens, is extremely tolerant of city conditions, but likes sun to produce many flowers. Five-leaved *Aralia* is a splendid foliage plant with no particular soil requirements and a propensity for shade. Some of the better bush honeysuckles, like *Lonicera fragrantissima* (almost an evergreen) and *L. tartarica,* bloom well in light shade and have red berries.

Vines for City Planting

Vines are invaluable in city gardens because of room. Trained along fences, walls, or up the sides of a house, they can serve as a protective screen as well as supplying good background for a garden. With a shrub or tree placed several feet in front of them, they give the illusion of depth. Oddly enough it isn't always seeing a whole vista that accentuates depth. Trying to see behind something planted part of the way down suggests more than there is. That is what is needed in a city or any other small garden.

Grapevines grow well almost anywhere. With plenty of humus their leaves are large and lovely of outline, their boldness a good contrast to smaller leaves in front. They even supply grapes if there is enough sun. In winter, with stout viney branches held fast to a fence, they are interesting patterns; and in spring, the reaching tendrils and new pink tips are a joy.

Ivy is fine used anywhere if kept within bounds. It is a

better ground-cover for many city yards than grass. Imprisoned between underground, steel walls 4–6″ high, it can serve as a border for a grass plot, a small garden, or a pebble terrace. Pots of it set high can drape an ugly wall in no time. Or it will grow up a wall from pots or good soil. Once established, it can fend for itself.

A city dweller has the same problem with vines as the country dweller — they grow too fast. Bittersweet, which bears berries in the shade (providing there are both sexes) must be pruned to keep it from taking over fence, wall, or terrace. But it's graceful and smoke-resistant. Fleece Vine *(Polygonum auberti)* is daintier but just as rampant. It produces a wealth of fragrant blossoms in late summer, and is indifferent to city hardships. Wisteria will climb from a struggling city garden, its blossoms hanging high up along a wall where the sun strikes for only a few hours a day.

From background, or skeleton plantings, provided by vines and flat shrubs, try experimenting with more unusual shrubs and a few perennials. Hostas, Day-Lilies, Pansies, and Forget-Me-Nots would do well for a beginning. Branch from there to Astilbe, Wild Blue Phlox, Garden Phlox, Siberian Iris, Ageratum, and others. Even Petunias are worth a try if they are not the fancy frilly kinds. Simple varieties are more apt to stand poor conditions.

Sometimes you must rely on potted plants because your backyard is a brick terrace. Try to eliminate enough of the bricks around the edge to plant a few vines, or tolerant shrubs, as a background for your pot plants. Properly played up, the humblest house plant can be dramatized. Wrongly treated, Coleus, Sansevieria and Croton are pathetic excuses for plants. Pot them in good soil, surround them with green-

(Gottscho-Schleisner)

A pool in a city garden.

ery and any of the three could become a good focal point. Begonias and Patience plants offer possibilities for flowers.

As a first step toward making something of your city backyard, rake it. Trim existing shrubbery neatly. If you have no compost to turn into the soil, use peat moss. It comes in large bales and is handy to store. Most nurseries rely on it entirely for building an acid soil. Set in plants, and mulch with peat moss; or cultivate around existing plants and mulch. The whole yard will begin to look spruced up. You'll want to buy new furniture or paint the old. For potted plants use the same size containers and paint them to blend with your house or garden furniture. Attention to a few details can go a long way toward making an attractive city yard.

THE POOL GARDEN

Have a pool in your garden even if it is only an old bathtub, a kitchen sink, or a metal half-barrel. Any of these can be painted a lovely blue-green on the inside, surrounded by a few flat rocks, and fitted into the general garden scheme so it looks natural and decorative. In this pool, parts of the sky or branches can be reflected. Ferns and wild flowers can surround it. Frogs can sport in it and gold fish streak through its waters to give an added note of color and pleasure. It can serve as a focal point to your garden. Sometimes a bit of water is just what is needed — to bring a garden together.

Birds love a bit of water. On the practical side, so do dogs and other animals, so we must build our pools in practical places. Camouflaging the edges with rocks is one way to discourage the pool from being used too frequently as a dog bath, and to restrain small children. Building it in a secluded spot is another. Or we can exchange natural fragrance for dog-repellant around plants in the area to discourage four-legged visitors.

Many times large boulders have shallow depressions in them that suggest they become bird-baths. Trailing Ivies, Sedums, and other shallow-rooted plants can tangle at its edge where the boulder goes underground and there is not much soil depth. Nearby Siberian Iris, Coral Bells, and deeper-rooted plants can help build a lovely spring picture, with other neighboring rocks and rock-garden plants completing the attractive ledge-outcropping.

Garden pools are not difficult to make. A simple one has the soil and subsoil excavated to a depth of 4–6 inches beyond the size desired, a layer of small stones lining the cavity, and two layers of cement poured over the stones.

The first layer of cement is composed of about three parts clean sand and gravel, and one part Portland cement. Mix it thoroughly. Slowly add water so that it becomes of a consistency that can be worked without being sloppy. You might have to work a little of it around the stones to try it out. Apply with a trowel so that the first layer covers the stones. Lay chicken wire over this to reinforce the concrete so that it won't crack. Allow to dry for three days, watering it down each day. The second layer, mixed with two parts sand and one part cement to a workable consistency, is applied to the depth of 1–2 inches after the first layer has "seasoned." Some people add a thin third coating of plain cement and water, colored blue or green.

Each layer should be laid without interruption, working from the center outward. If the atmosphere is very dry, cover layers with a cloth to retain moisture and to keep them from drying too quickly. The overall thickness of the pool bottom should be 4–6 inches. If there is to be an outlet, the drain

A pool at the bottom of a sunken garden.

pipe must be laid and cemented before the bottom layer of stones is arranged.

Pools can be made any shape desired. A kidney-shaped pool or one of irregular outline seems to fit in best with an informal garden or woodsy area. A round pool fits in any-where. Rectangular pools seems to be the ones most used in formal gardens. They are usually made with forms, and are of more elaborate construction than a small round one, but rectangular steel pools which can be bought are easily assembled.

However, for the purposes of the home-owner whose yard is small, the pool described above is quite adequate. One sloping gradually from the sides, with the deepest part in the center, is the safest to have with young children around. A depth of 18–24 inches is adequate for a water lily.

Lilies and other plants can be planted right in the bottom, in rich soil covered with sand, or in special containers (large flower pots or small tubs). Hardy plants will live out all winter if the water is left in and deep enough so that the roots won't freeze. Some of the aquatic plants need shallower water than lilies. For them, special pockets in the shallower parts of the pool can be built right in with the construction.

Do not plant acid-loving plants next to the pool for at least the first season because of the lime in the cement. For the same reason no fish should be allowed in the pool until it has been dried thoroughly, and soaked a few times, and dried again. Once filled with water and planted however, a pool can remain virtually untouched for two years, water being added during dry spells, and the correct balance of fish, snails and other "cleaning" agents keep the pool clean. Oxygenating plants that glamourize water depths are not necessary to the outdoor pool, but they help keep the water clean, promote interest, and become undulating foliage screens to protect baby fish. Algae grows in any still water, so don't let it alarm you; there will be far less in a shady pool than in the sun.

In autumn, keep leaves from collecting in the water by laying chicken wire over the top of the pool. If the water is at least 2' deep, and fish and lilies remain out all winter, cover the pool with boards, or lay one or two boards in the water to break the hard freezing of ice. If it is a shallow pool, bring fish indoors with a few oxygenating plants and other tender aquatics, and keep in a large aquarium. When warm weather comes again the pool can be cleaned and replanted, or have water added to the proper depth before fish and plants are set in.

Don't overload your pool, although it's fun to try plants totally different from those with which you are familiar. Send for a catalogue of pool specialties and study the characteristics of water plants that appeal to you. If your pool is small you wouldn't want grassy leaves growing out of it to 6' and more. The fat balloons of Water Hyacinth are fun to have bouncing on top of a pool, but so eager is it to populate the world with its own importance that small surfaces are soon obliterated.

A tub garden consisting of one tub or very small pool, should contain no more than one small Water Lily of the pygmy type and perhaps one other aquatic of an upright nature. This could be Umbrella Palm *(Cyperus alternifolius)* with a parasol of palm-like leaves to shade the water. A larger pool can support more plants, arranged artistically with due regard to contrast of foliage and height and with plenty of water showing. Three tubs can be planted as a unit, with bog plants around and between, and rocks set in various places to tie the water areas together.

Try to plan your shady pool garden so that there will be sun enough on the water for at least one lily. At the edges, the shade-tolerant plants can be used, low growing ones nearest the water, with taller accents here and there. If it is a large pool or swamp area, you'll enjoy such things as Red Lobelia and Jewel-Weed *(Impatiens pallida)* several feet from the water area, with native Inkberry, Sweet Pepper-Bush, prickly Holly in the background. A man-made pool should have higher plants in back of the pool, particularly some evergreens, so the pool garden and low plants around it will be shown to the best advantage.

Following is a partial list of aquatic and bog plants tolerant of some shade, and suitable for natural ponds or home-made pools. Try one or two different kinds each year.

Aquatics and Oxygenating Plants for the Outdoor Pool

Acorus calamus — Sweet-Flag. To 6'. Deep pools. Half-shade. Attractive narrow grassy foliage; inconspicuous flowers.

Alisma — Water-Plantain. Attractive heart-shaped leaves. Branching spikes of white flowers tinged with pink. Streams and bog margins in partial shade.

Aponogeton distachyus — Water-Hawthorn, because of sweet-supposedly Hawthorn-like fragrance. Flat, floating leaves. Twin spires of bloom, almost incessant. Light shade. Deep water.

Cabomba — Fanwort. Oxygenating plant. Fan-like leaves below the surface. Other leaves float. Hardy to Baltimore if roots don't freeze. Must be planted in soil. Does not like lime.

Calla palustris — Water-Calla. To 12″. Like miniature Calla-

Lily. Blossom, a white spathe surrounding a yellow spadix. Red berries in August. Half-shade; shallow water.

Caltha palustris — Marsh-Marigold. Shiny, Buttercup-like blossoms in spring. Good foliage. Likes wet places near water, but does well in rich soil full of humus. Hardy; prefers semi-shade.

Cyperus alternifolius — Umbrella-Palm. Dwarf variety most used. To 18″. Resembles miniature clump of Palm Trees. Rich soil. Shallow water. Not hardy but will live over indoors with wet roots.

Eichhornea crassipes — Water-Hyacinth. Beautiful lavendar spikes of flowers practically all summer. Odd balloon-like leaves. Can be anchored in shallow water or float on top. Increases rapidly. Not hardy.

Elodea — *(Anacharis canadensis)* — Water-Thyme. Oxygenating plant to 4′, depending on the depth of water. Pretty and graceful.

Hydrocleys nymphoides — Water-Poppy. Showy leaves that float on water. Yellow, Poppy-like flowers blooming almost continuously. Prefers sun, but does well in light shade. Shallow water. Not hardy but fun to grow.

Iris pseudacorus — Yellow-Flag Iris. 2—3′. Large graceful clumps. Bog conditions. Tolerates half-shade.

Jussiaea longifolia — Primrose-Willow. To 2′. Narrow pointed leaves. Profuse yellow flowers in summer. Damp soil or shallow water. Light shade. *J. repens.* Partially submerged vine. Yellow flowers. Neither variety hardy.

Lemna — Duckweed. Minute, floating aquatic plants of bright green. Can be gathered from almost any pond. Fish like them.

Ludwigia. Oxygenating plant. Foliage lined with pink. Likes shade.

Marsilea Drummondi — Four-leaf Water-Clover. Floats on water, but will grow in wet soil. Half-shade.

Menyanthes trifoliata — Bogbean. Native of cool bogs. Fragrant white blossoms on stout stalks. Half-shade.

Myriophyllum proserpinacoides — Parrots-Feather. Feathery foliage of numerous whorls of leaves. Must be planted in soil. Foliage growing out of water is particularly lovely. Tolerates light shade.

Myosotis scorpiodes or *M. cespitosa* — True Forget-Me-Not. Appealing little sky-blue flowers with yellow eyes. Shallow water, but grows in dryer areas. Blooms almost all summer.

Nasturtium officinale — Water-Cress. Hardy, trailing European perennial easily naturalized in pools and streams. Bright foliage. Sharp, piquant flavor.

Nymphoides peltatum — Floating-Heart. Waterlily-like leaves. Bright yellow flowers June to August. Shallow water. Best confined to tub of rich soil because of spreading habit. Hardy.

Pistia stratiotes — Water-Lettuce. Tender perennial of Arum Family. Floating rosettes of pale green leaves, velvety to the touch, decorative, feathery roots. Shade. Warm pools and ponds.

Pontederia cordata — Pickerel-Weed. To 1' above water. Hardy native. Bold, arrow-shaped leaves. Spikes of violet-blue blossoms carried well above the water. Blooms July–August. Half-shade. Shallow water.

Sagittaria engelmanniana or *S. latifolia* — Arrow-Head. Hardy native. Heart-shaped leaves. Pretty, clustered white flowers. Shallow water. Tolerates light shade.

Saururus cernuus — Lizards-Tail. 2–5'. Hardy perennial. Shallow water. Dense, terminal spike of small fragrant flowers. July–August. Light shade.

Typha — Cat-Tail. To 10'. Flat, narrow leaves. Blunt spikes of brown flowers. Bogs or swamp. For large areas. Light shade.

Vallisneria — Eel-Grass.   Oxygenating   perennials.   Long, slender leaves. Tiny, 3-petaled flowers, white, carried to surface of the water on spiral stalks.

Oxygenating plants differ from most aquatic plants in that they grow under water, rather than on top. They absorb impurities from the water, liberate oxygen, help clarify the water, and shelter baby fish. Most are better planted by themselves (not with lilies etc.) in soil, though some will live floating in the water.

14

Mulches and Maintenance

✦❈✦✦❈✦✦❈✦✦❈✦✦❈✦✦❈✦✦❈✦✦❈✦✦❈✦✦❈✦✦❈✦✦❈✦✦❈✦

MULCHING is so definitely a part of garden economy these days that it comes first in any discussion of maintenance. Although the ground does not dry out so quickly in a shady garden, nor do the weeds seem to grow so fast, adding a summer mulch after cultivating saves so much time, energy and discouragement that any gardener attempting an attractive garden without plenty of help would do well to try it.

Summer mulching is covering the top of the soil with a substance to keep down the weeds and keep in the moisture. It does both with surprising and wonderful efficiency.

Mulching materials vary according to the part of the country one lives in. In some places peanut, buckwheat, and other hulls are abundant and inexpensive. In others, straw and corn products can be had. Sawmills in the North and East are trying to promote sawdust as a mulch. In addition, gardeners have used at various times, stones, paper, peat moss, marsh hay, tobacco refuse, pine needles, grass clippings, even weeds.

Around shrubs, trees, and in other areas where the mulch is not desired for building up the soil too, ground cornhusks, sugar cane, sawdust, wood chips, pine needles and other coarse products applied to a depth of 3–4 inches keep their form as a mulch for several seasons. Around perennials and show gardens, finer products like peat moss and buckwheat hulls make a better appearance. Needles of white pine can be used in either case. In Chapter 9 I spoke of charming seashore places where whole yards were covered with pine needles, leaving only the garden spaces free. With no lawn to mow, you can devote more time to cultivating.

Peat moss still impresses me as the best all-around mulch, its only drawback being that the fine kinds mat together so that it repels water rather than absorbing it. But it gives a neat, well-kept appearance, simulating soil, and in time becomes a part of the soil.

People invariably infer that peat moss, oak leaves and pine needles make a soil too acid. Most plants don't care about the acidity of the soil; a great number must have it acid, while only a few like alkaline conditions. Around those few dig in wood ashes or a little ground limestone. The important thing is to get compost into the soil and not to worry about acidity.

Here is a good system of cultivating and mulching. In March, April, and early May, nothing much need be done in shady gardens except to rake off the leaves— their natural winter mulch — and dump them on the compost pile. As Narcissus and Tulip foliage die down, and all the late come-uppers are spotted, cultivate lightly and mulch with peat moss or other good mulching material. Work small areas at a time, leaving them neat and orderly until the whole garden is gone over. If a plant has to be moved (such as

moving late-blooming white Narcissi under a white Dogwood), choose a rainy day in spring to do it. The same thing
applies to separating late-blooming plants like Blue Lobelia
and Monkshood. All of these are mulched afterward. If you
decide to move something *after* it has been mulched, move
the mulch aside and replace it. Once mulched with pine
needles, however, an area is usually done for the season.

In my shady rock garden (high shade, practically no sun),
where only excess leaves are removed from the permanent
compost-mulch, I turn in new compost around plants as they
need it. This year it might be some hosta and *Galax*. Next
year it might be a clump of garden Phlox, or Tansies, that
need separating in late summer.

Work from the most noticeable parts of the garden to
those that don't show so much, leaving some areas bare for
annuals. When these are set in (around the first of June),
allow them to get a good start and then mulch them. By the
middle of June everything should be in order and the garden
look attractive. Garden duties become those of staking, spraying as little as possible, cutting off dead flower heads, a little
weeding and edging.

Toward the end of July the peat moss part of the garden
needs light cultivating and weeding, some possible feeding,
and remulching, either with more peat moss or with pine
needles. Late August and early September is time for separating some plants (a few spring flowers are separated earlier).
Remove pine needles, dig up, reset the plant using ½-bushel
of humus in the process, and remulch. Peat moss mulch can
now be dug in.

By mid-autumn the pine needles are entirely removed
from most garden areas and piled in large mounds in various
spots convenient for use next year. The reason they are not

left on the garden for the winter is that they should not mix any more than they do anyhow with the oak leaves which fall onto all the garden, making a natural winter mulch. Pine needles take years to decompose.

All this moving and re-moving of pine needles may seem like a lot of work. It is — but it is not as much as the weeding and cultivating would be if the mulching *wasn't* done. Those few extra minutes in spring are worth many a golden hour later when you might be enjoying your shady garden at the height of a heat wave and not slaving over weeds. By systematic cultivating and permanent mulching, whole yards can gradually be brought under control until they stay comparatively neat with a minimum of attention.

Mulching does not do away with the work of gardening. Weeds do come up through the mulch and have to be pulled out; mulches must be replenished, but everything is so much easier to manage. The ground stays comparatively cool and aerated, plants remain fresh looking, and flower beds appear neat and well cared for.

Fall mulching for winter coverage and protection often does more harm than good. It is apt to freeze or smother plants. Early mulching allows rodents to get in and harm the plants. A garden under deciduous trees actually does not need to be covered. Leaves drifting down through the autumn days form a natural and safe winter mulch. Rely on nature's protection; only in a few instances do you need to add to it.

First, around plants that might winter-kill or where the soil is very hard, turn in more compost — one of the last fall duties. This breaks up the soil so that there is less chance of its freezing and thawing. Many times when we say a plant winter-killed, it is actually that the roots were exposed during various freezing processes and the plant died.

Rough compost added to the soil in the autumn assures better drainage. In a heavy soil particularly, water is apt to stand and freeze on plants. Not many plants can live through such an experience. Rotted manure added as a light mulch late in the season acts the same as compost. Too much manure might keep the ground too warm and start lush, unseasonal growth. Always keep manure away from plant stems.

Around Christmas time visit the garden if there is no snow, to see where leaves have fallen. After the holiday use Christmas tree and other evergreen boughs — which protect but let in air — for further coverage of tender plants. These are plants whose leaves are apt to burn in the winter sun and wind — Arbutus, *Galax, Shortia galacifolia,* Ivy, etc. This burning, if allowed to continue, eventually so weakens a plant that it dies. And burned foliage is unsightly in the early spring garden. Covering Ivy, *Mahonia,* Arbutus, etc., keeps leaves fresh and green so that they look attractive when the covering is removed. In your garden, your experience will soon become your guide.

In spring, the leaves should be raked off gradually; first, the top layers in areas where the leaves lie thickest; then entirely from around hardy bulbs and spring-blooming perennials. Tender plants should have the leaves around them loosened so that air and light can penetrate, then gradually removed so that when danger of heavy frost is over, the garden is clean.

Moisture is one of the essentials of growing plants, freeing nutrients in the soil so that delicate roots can absorb them. Although trees protect the soil in a shady garden and keep it from drying out too quickly, many of the shady plants are those requiring a lot of moisture. Even if your garden looks well and prosperous, *know* when it is getting dry between rains, and water it. Give it a thorough soaking before you go away for a vacation. If it is well-mulched, it should remain in good condition for several weeks.

During the past few years droughts have occurred in parts of the country where they were hitherto not considered natural. Water shortages, or a drain on a community's water-system, which has not had time to catch up with growth in population, have forced many towns to issue restrictions on the use of water. The value of mulching thus is further emphasized. Mulching cuts the necessity of watering to a half or a third.

Because of droughts you may have to reorganize your watering habits, doing it thoroughly and systematically, one small portion of the garden each day, taking a week or ten days to get around the whole garden. This thorough watering is good; shallow watering is apt to encourage shallow roots, and they dry out quickly in droughts. Therefore, encourage the roots of plants to dig deep into the soil by not watering at all during spring and early summer, until absolutely necessary. (Naturally, this does not apply to newly planted grass areas or where annuals have just been set out.) So, it's deep, infrequent watering instead of frequent shallow sprinkling. This saves time as well as energy and water.

Using a watering can is never prohibited, and special plants need it in between times (those recently transplanted or separated, young trees, etc.) If the drought is very bad, make a series of moats around or in back of plants needing extra water and keep filling them up until the water has soaked down around the plant roots.

A word should be mentioned here about watering during

transplanting. The ideal time to transplant, separate or move anything in the garden is during or just after a rainy spell. Then extra watering is not necessary. If the ground is dry, however, water the plant before digging, add water to the hole before setting the plant in, water after planting, and mulch. Keep the soil moist until the plant is established and growing. Get it off to a good start. This even applies to Phlox and other perennials at the end of summer. Even though the tops die down, the roots are growing; and the better roots a plant can make before cold weather, the better plant you will have the following season.

One of the most important considerations in garden maintenance is edging. If the lawn is blurred into the flower garden or shrubbery group, it isn't clean-cut and orderly. A sharp edge defines and invariably means a neat yard, even though a lawn might be poor and weedy. Edging it once a season is usually enough.

If you don't like gardening, stick to the things you can reasonably take care of to have your home well planted. If you have a yen for flowers and shrubs, but not much time to devote to them, try to arrange them so that they demand as little work as possible. Don't have too many individual beds dotted about the lawn. Plant perennials, annuals, and bulbs around trees and shrubs already established. Or confine your gardening to shrubs which, once well-planted, need little further attention.

If your lot consists only of a lawn and a few trees, and your idea of a garden is an abundance of flowers, dig your flower beds where they will make sense, such as at the outside edge of a property or lawn, and where they will demand a minimum of care, be accessible to water, and in an area which you can enjoy.

The busy gardener can eliminate need for edging by setting in a low strip of steel, lawn high and practically

(Gottscho-Schleisner)

Brick or flagstone walks will do away with the edging problem.

invisible, at the edge of flower beds. In a similar manner, a brick edging can be sunk to grass level so that the grass need only be trimmed.

Brick or flagstone walks used between flower beds will do away with the grass edging problem altogether. They should be wide enough, however (3–6 feet), to show off the flowers to the best advantage. All paths should be easy to walk on, attractive and practical. Pine needles make excellent paths. Pebbles are good in certain shady areas as a contrast to plant materials, but they should be edged with something (like bricks) to keep them in place. Gravel is good to walk on but has to be weeded. Bricks are attractive. Cement is practical but stiff.

Shady areas, where grass is difficult to establish, can be turned into brick, flagstone, or other types of terraces, with a perennial or shrub border around the outside. Designs for many of the modern yards eliminate grass altogether, preferring paved areas for the sake of practicability. For decoration in these yards, one or two flower beds, built up a few feet for easy access and maintenance, fit in with the general modern design. To the mind of a gardener, this seems too strictly utilitarian. Stretches of green grass are enjoyable. Flower beds should not serve merely as architectural embellishment but be used for cutting purposes and other aesthetic pleasures. Trees should be loved for something besides just casting shadows where shadows are needed.

But the minimum-work gardener is another thing. He loves his flowers, often growing twice as many as he can take care of. He is always looking for short cuts and time savers because he is so ambitious, and there *are* short cuts and time savers which contribute toward an attractive garden. He would do well, for instance, to mulch or have a ground-cover under large specimen trees such as Maples and Beeches, and not try to grow grass there at all. Obvious paths across lawns should be treated as paths, by using stepping stones as a suggestive and often interesting detail. One can waste time battling with areas that won't grow grass, instead of solving the problem by recognizing it.

Turn liabilities into assets. Do you have a large boulder or stump in your lawn? Use growing plants (it will be no more difficult to mow around or edge), and make it the center of a plant picture. If it is a stump, and unattractive, plant Ivy or another vine that will completely cover it. The vine will keep the stump moist and cool so that it will rot more quickly.

Erect fences if and when they are needed, but have them attractive. Rustic fences go with rustic surroundings. Don't waste your fences. Plant sections of them to vines you have always wanted to grow. They will enhance the fence; the fence should enhance the vines. Use small, practical fences, suggestions of fences, or wire deterrents around plants that are being mutilated by children or dogs, before the plants are entirely destroyed.

Keeping a garden neat is part of gardening. Staking Phlox, Monkshood, Red Lobelia, and other tall-growing perennials, or those that the rain might knock down, should be done before they sprawl. Use substantial green stakes that won't be conspicuous. Use small bamboo or wire stakes for Snapdragons and other lower plants. Keep in mind the particular plants in your garden that will need staking from year to year.

Cut off dead flower heads. Cut tall, dead stalks way to the ground so stumps won't show. Lay Narcissus foliage on the ground when it begins to droop, and hold it down with stones. Let the sun get at it but keep it out of sight. The best you can do with Tulip foliage is to plant shrubby material in front of it. You can cut off flower heads of both, but the leaves are needed to make food to replenish the bulb. Keep faded flowers of Day-Lilies and other plants cut so that new buds will continue to grow. In this way the plants maintain their enthusiasm. Some time in July, cut back Pansies, Sweet Alyssum, etc., to stimulate new growth from the bottom. Plants in the shade must be kept looking better than average because so much depends on looks in a shady garden.

People often make too much of pruning. Gone is the day of the manicured basketballs. Nothing more need be done to evergreens than to cut off dead branches and prune them selectively, a branch taken off here and there to enhance their shapes. If an evergreen grows too large for its space within a few years, it should not have been planted there. Knowing the ultimate height and manner of growth of shrubs before planting helps in selecting the right one. Such things as Laurel, Umbrella Pine, both Andromedas, and a few of the yews are slow growing and should be used in confined areas instead of taller growing shrubs that have to be pruned.

Evergreens can be pruned moderately at Christmas and the branches used for decoration. Yet too drastic pruning during the winter is not good, particularly in a dry climate. If an evergreen must be topped or sheared (as Hemlock for a hedge), the best time to do it is spring or early summer.

Late summer and autumn pruning might induce new growth, which would die in the winter and weaken the shrub.

Deciduous shrubs are treated differently, but with the same theory of keeping the shrub to its natural shape. Rampant growers like some Viburnums, Forsythia, Beauty-Bush, etc., should be planted where they'll have room to spread. Even so, if they like the soil, they'll often have to be pruned — and drastically.

The ideal for many deciduous, spring-blooming shrubs is to keep them young, encouraging new shoots to grow from the bottom, and to remove an old stalk every two or three years. Good pruning is thinning out rather than cutting back. Take out weak branches from the center of the shrub and prune back sucker-like growths from stems, which detract from its shape. Always cut to a stem or leaf bud, to hide the stub. Prune new branches only to shape the shrub, remembering that the more new branches taken, the less bloom you are apt to have. Young branches have the most actively growing buds.

Learn the habits of your shrubs. Forsythia sometimes grows so rampantly that drastic pruning is inevitable. Make it make sense. Prune in the winter to bring branches in to force in the house. Consider it pruning when you cut the blooming branches, choosing those which need to be eliminated. Forsythia foliage can be used in summer too, yet with all this cutting, extra pruning is often needed. Do it right after the bush has bloomed. Deutzias grow rampantly too, with much dying back of old wood. In fact, they are so woody as to be hardly worth planting in the modern scheme of functional decorations.

Sweet Pepper-Bush, a summer bloomer, is well worth cultivating, with a neat habit of coming up from the bottom to form a clump. It only needs the pruning of dead wood, of which there is little, and suckers pulled out if they outgrow their bonds. Azaleas usually bloom rampantly on vigorous young growth, which should be encouraged. Cut out very old branches unless the bush has developed to tree size and there are no suckers.

Nurserymen are apt to top a bush or tree when selling it to you, particularly if it is late in the season for moving it. Then it is up to you — the new grower — to reclaim the plant's natural shape by additional pruning to bring out graceful lines. Cutting back of a shrub is good for the plant when it is moved, for a shrub should have only as much top growth as the roots can support. If the roots are cut or torn in transit, the top growth must be cut back to match them.

Invest in the best clippers you can find with which to do your pruning. Proper tools have a great deal to do with good cultivating and easy maintenance of a garden. They don't have to be fancy, or expensive; they do have to be of strong construction. A spade or shovel should be of the right heft. Try it — lift it — see if it feels right in your hands before buying it. If you're a woman, don't automatically buy the lightest tools. Often they are not worth the cost, for they don't do the proper work. Long handled shovels are easier to work with and easier on backs.

Tools don't have to be numerous. A spade, a shovel (or both), a durable scratcher, a sturdy trowel, a watering can, and pruners will take care of a good-sized ornamental garden. One of the best investments is a little carryall cart. It is much easier to manage than a wheelbarrow, has excellent balance, and its large wheel rubber tires enable you to pull it anywhere.

The magazines are full of advertisements for all sorts of

time and energy savers. In all fairness, you will have to try things yourself. Many of the new products are good. Perhaps you'll find that they actually do save time and energy, but there are so many gadgets being thrown at us these days that I am skeptical and wary. I like a little muscle stretching with my gardening. I love the digging and planting. To date I haven't seen any weed killer as effective as two hands, except for such things as poison ivy. I haven't heard of any good substitute for animal manure and compost. It's a day of gadgets, but most of them are more trouble to use than the effort they save. And anyway, I like the effort.

15

Preyers and Sprayers

✥✣✥✣✥✣✥✣✥✣✥✣✥✣✥✣✥✣✥✣✥✣✥✣✥✣✥✣✥✣✥✣

EVERY SILVER LINING has a cloud, gardening is no exception; the cloud in this instance being numerous pests and diseases. How aphids, lace bugs, borers, rose chafers, Japanese beetles, chinch bugs, tent caterpillars, red spiders, cyclamen mites, leaf hoppers, and a host of others find their way into the choicest sections of the garden is beyond the ken of a mere gardener. But they do. Are we to go on using more powerful sprays in ever increasing quantities and encourage bigger, better and more resistant insects? Or are we to make our plants as healthy as possible, spray as little as we can get away with, and enjoy less perfect plants?

How and why do diseases attack our plants? We can dose them with more and more drugs, lessen their resistance so that they're ready for the next type of fungus, rust, blight, leaf spot, mosaic, mildew, and the only thing left is to dig them up and burn them. Or we can make them as healthy as possible and "treat" them only when absolutely necessary, letting a few leaves and buds die on less perfect plants.

How important *is* perfection of each blossom and leaf? No one appreciates any more than I the exquisite formation of waxy petals without a blemish; or of shiny foliage, well-kept and beautifully formed. Perfection is what we strive for and yet — is it actually what we want? We might be bored if our plants were absolutely free of pests and diseases. The struggle to keep them in good condition (if not *too* disheartening) adds to our appreciation of what perfection we achieve.

I am not an organic gardener, with hidebound beliefs that all composting and no spraying, makes a healthy plant. I am for spraying, but only when it is absolutely necessary. My theory in raising by garden-children is the same as in bringing up human children. Make them healthy, build up their natural resistance. and call in extreme measures when all else fails.

Many factors enter into the health and resistance of a plant; nutrients in the soil, availability of those nutrients (including the condition of the soil), climate, weather, location (latitude, longitude, even the location in the individual garden), prevalence of pests and diseases in the neighborhood, right amount of shade and sunlight, fertilization, moisture, temperature, and, in general, whether or not a plant likes its particular spot. We can't possibly satisfy the demands of all our plants since they are from various parts of the world and demand entirely different growing conditions.

Plants must like where they are growing. I was talking with a woman about her Fuschias that were 10 feet or so from their last year's home. My friend shook her head. "Nope, they're not happy. They need a little more shade — just the amount they had last year."

Like human beings, plants that are not "happy" fall an easy prey to pests and diseases. Sometimes they just seem to dry up. As the soil improves, the plants improve, followed by health and resistance to diseases and pests. A weak plant, like a weak person, is usually the first to succumb to infestations and epidemics. Using composted materials will not eliminate all threat of cutworms, or of other pests, and diseases, but it does strengthen the plants so that they are not so apt to fall prey to them.

Laurel bushes like an acid soil. Arbovitae trees are happiest growing in rich woodlands. Planted where it is too hot, dry, and sunny, they suffer from red spider. Rhododendrons, too crowded or in too much sun, invite lace bugs. Fir trees are happier in cool, high altitudes. And so it goes, the demands of each individual plant sometimes so different from those of its neighbor that the plants cannot survive near each other, sometimes so similar as to seem the same.

I had read that herbs and geraniums in a garden discourage rose bugs and other insects. Herbs are an added attraction and useful. Thymes of various varieties I planted between the stepping stones of my rose terrace. Geraniums were placed on the steps. At either side of a *Pyracantha*, two Lavender bushes were planted; nearby, a Poterium. For the second season fewer rose bugs are found here, while in another part of the garden, where there are no herbs, the rose bugs swarm over Shasta Daisies, Peonies, and Astilbes, and there seems to be a greater number of other pests.

The following paragraphs may interest you if you are reaching for any "straw" that might discourage pests and lessen the spraying schedule. Herbs are not basically shade-tolerant (though some will grow in light shade) but perhaps your shady garden is near enough a sunny area for you to grow a few.

Pyrethrum *(Chrysanthemum coccineum)*, a pretty daisy-like perennial whose dried blossoms form the base of Pyrethrum spray, is repulsive to aphids, lace bugs, thrips and other insects. The plant, even while growing, gives off a gas that is deadly to certain small insects.

With a sense of smell far more acute than that of man, insects are sensitive to odors that we cannot even detect or that we rather enjoy. Lavender, for instance, has long been used in clothes and linen closets as a moth-repellent.

Tobacco, the source of nicotine (a deadly contact and stomach poison for many insects), is another deterrent in its natural state. The refuse can be ground and used as a mulch to discourage root-aphids and other pests, as well as rabbits and dogs. Tobacco refuse mulch can later be worked into the soil to add soil nutrients (2–4 percent nitrogen, 4–10 percent potash, and a little phosphorus) and help condition the soil.

The plant world holds many possibilities. In various tests, oil from Sweet Basil *(Ocimum basilicum)* killed 95 percent of mosquito larvae in a certain area. An extract made from American Chestnut *(Castanea dentata)* is a good repellent against Japanese beetle. Coriander *(Coriandrum sativum)* contains an oil that is dangerous to certain insects. An old reference to Virginia creeper *(Parthenocissus quinquefolia)* states that a bunch of its leaves rubbed onto an infested area of an apple tree made the tree free from aphids for weeks afterward. As usual, the old adage holds true: one man's (or insect's) meat is another's poison. The job is to find something that is harmless to man, household pets, and beneficial insects; but has the ability to kill pests and deter animals.

In the case of plant diseases (rots, rusts, blights, etc.), soil fertility — or lack of it — plays a large part. Oddly enough, the richer some soils are in certain basic nutrients, the sooner certain crops are apt to fall prey to disease. If wheat growing in moderately fertile soil is given extra nitrogen, it is apt to become subject to root rot, rust, and mildew though it escapes seedling diseases. Nitrogen fertilizers harm pine and other conifer seedlings. Too much nitrogen in the soil promotes wilt diseases. Where there is not enough potash and phosphorus, root rot is apt to occur, the stimulation of the green growth by the nitrogen being too much for the inadequate development of the roots, which need potash and phosphorus. The addition of barnyard manure to soils growing potatoes often causes scab, which can be avoided by growing potatoes in an acid soil.

Most experiments along these lines have been in the agricultural field, but many of the theories are applicable to decorative plants. When we read that the country is using twice as much lime and commercial fertilizer as before World War II, and that there is less barnyard manure and fewer green crops being turned into the soil, we cannot help wondering how much the lack of organic matter in the soil has to do with the prevalence of plant diseases and the spread of insects. Are the organic gardeners right when they suggest that too much spraying with harmful insecticides and fungicides has killed off birds, frogs, snakes, and beneficial insects — the natural enemies of many garden pests — so that our plants and crops are overrun? Are they right when they intimate that with lack of organic material soils have not been replenished enough to support plants so that they fall easy prey to diseases? Are they right in advocating no spraying and only organic fertilizers? Perhaps there is a happy medium of building up soil with organic material, supplementing it with chemical fertilzer when you know your soil is deficient, and spraying just enough to keep insects and diseases under control.

I prefer the last suggestion and I have a reasonably happy garden. A few leaves are eaten; occasionally there is a bout with mildew or rust; but these are not noticeable as one smells the fragrance of a Lily, or marvels at the design of a Coleus leaf, or enjoys the refreshing coolness under the shifting shadows of Oak boughs and evergreen branches.

In the past, what did men do without the many chemical sprays and fertilizers that we have today? Undoubtedly, conditions were better then. The early days were days of virgin soil when crop insects had not had time to congregate and reproduce to today's vast multitudes.

Several hundred years ago farming and gardening were not so intensive. With fewer people and more land, and consequently more "wild" plants for them to feed on, insects did not have to attack cultivated areas. Fewer insects meant also fewer diseases, for many diseases are carried by insects.

Today we have more species of insects in America. It has been said that of the seventy-three of our worst insect pests, thirty-seven originally came from foreign countries. They have come on plants, animals, and men; by ship and by air. They have also arrived by themselves. The bollweevil and Harlequin bug, for instance, have worked their way up from Mexico as parts of our Southwestern desert (once a barrier to these insects) have been reclaimed. Some, like the gypsy moth, have been brought here for experimental purposes. We have found out too late that, without their native predators, they become menaces.

There have always been pests and diseases of some sort. We read of grasshopper and locust plagues. There is the Biblical story of the prophet Amos, a "dresser of sycamores," who climbed sycamore trees to pinch off the ends of the young fruit which resembled figs, hoping this would destroy the insects found there.

This and other references lead us to believe that man has always had some trouble in growing plants. He might not have worried so much about it, for many crops he picked along the roadsides, knowing not how to grow them, but where the crops grew naturally. Years ago, many people lived principally on meat and fish. Roots and herbs served mostly as garnishes and flavorings, as well as for medicines, tonics, and fragrances.

What control of insects and diseases there was, was mostly guesswork, but as far back as 1681 we hear of arsenical compounds being used. Two hundred years later, came the first record of effective chemical control. A Frenchman, Millardet, sprayed his grape vines with a bluish mixture of lime and copper sulphate to simulate a poison, and prevent people from stealing his fruit. Not long after this he reported that this same Bordeaux Mixture protected the plants from mildew. We are still using it.

An American Journal of Science in 1825 tells of boring a hole into the heart of a "fine large shady tree in Albany . . . so infested with worms and caterpillars that passers-by were obliged to make a circuit to avoid it. . . ." The hole was filled with sulphur, and plugged, and in forty-eight hours the tree was rid of pests.

A few years later (about 100 years ago) people became so worried about the increase in insect damage that Townsend Glover, an entomologist, was employed by the government.

That same year Asa Fitch became the first State Entomologist in New York. The Colorado potato-beetle was one of the first worries; Paris Green was one of the first arsenicals. "From then on the race between new pests and new insecticides was close, with the depredations of the insects always a bit greater each year. . . ."

With the development of Rotenone, Pyrethrum, Nicotine, and others, a great step forward was realized by the spray industry. These were not enough; insect population jumped as more food was demanded to be grown in less space by fewer people. This was a further challenge to the insecticide industry (over a $100,000,000 industry at the beginning of World War II); with Pyrethrum and Rotenone ingredients difficult to import under war conditions, organic insecticides came into their own. DDT was the great discovery.

But DDT, along with killing the obnoxious pests also killed off many of their natural enemies, so that our plants still suffered but in a different way. For the past year or so DDT has been played down, though it is still being used. Further investigations are being made so that its place in the insecticide field can be determined and people won't use it indiscriminately. In the meantime, other more toxic insecticides and fungicides are being advertised. People are cautioned against breathing their deadly fumes or allowing parts of their bodies to come into contact with them.

Parathion (the most deadly of them all) kills the obnoxious Japanese beetles and rose bugs, but it is closely related to the nerve gases of the war and is death to fish, frogs, toads, bees and other beneficial insects; and it requires special handling in both its manufacture and usage. The pleasure rather goes out of hobby-gardening when one has to sally forth on a spraying expedition garbed in hat, raincoat, and gloves kept especially for the purpose, plus a respirator which is suggested in using parathion. I like frogs and tadpoles in my pool, and toads and beneficial insects in the garden. I like the birds to feed on the insects. (Birds too seem fewer, but there are no statistics available.) These smaller animals go to make up part of garden enjoyment. They belong with the flowers and trees. And yet, I have seen no toads in my seven acres of garden and woods for the past three years; and out of dozens of lively frogs in my woodland pool, there was one left this year after the air-spraying.

Air-spraying is still in its infancy, but from all I can read, it is becoming the preferred method of treating large areas. Less material is wasted; it is more efficient and they say less upsetting to nature. Over 3,000,000 acres in New England were sprayed by air for gypsy moth. The amount of DDT used in the spraying (one-half lb. per acre) should not have been enough to kill frogs and other small animals unless there was an overlap in the spraying. Beekeepers were warned and special precautions were taken about ponds, rivers, and other fish areas. Small pools suffered.

In the home garden the person who likes to enjoy plants and flowers with a minimum of effort, and who is relatively unaware of the seriousness of infestations and the chemicals that control them, must rely on what he is sold at the stores. More and more this is coming to mean all-purpose sprays, a number of which are on the market and fairly successful. However, even the best combination sprays mean some over-spraying, which is not particularly good.

Gardeners would do well to understand at least a little about combating certain plant diseases and pests. Sucking insects puncture and suck juices from stems and leaves; aphids of various colors are the most prevalent. Others are scale insects, lace bugs, spider mites (called red spiders), thrips, leaf hoppers. These can be exterminated by any good contact insecticide, which must hit and smother them in order to be effective. Some of these are pyrethrum, rotenone, nicotine sulphate; and the dangerous DDT, malathion, and parathion. You will probably buy any or several of these ingredients in combination, but look at the label to see that the package contains the material to do the job at hand.

Chewing insects make large holes in both foliage and flowers, even in tough Rhododendron leaves. They may be any of hundreds of insects such as Colorado potato beetles, rose chafers, Japanese beetles, bagworm, cutworms, slugs (included among which are the slimy larvae of some beetles), and earwigs which are now devasting northern gardens. Most of them can be controlled with stomach poisons, sprayed on leaves and flower buds before they open, so that insects are poisoned as they eat. Rotenone, lead arsenate, chlordane (dusted or watered into the soil to kill the grub of beetles) malathion, DDT, parathion are a few of the stomach poisons, which can be included in the spray that you purchase.

Sober reflection on all the diseases liable to attack shrubs and flowers is enough to discourage anyone from gardening. Soils deficient in certain necessary elements are often the causes of disease. This bears complete study and experiment, if one is earning a living from growing plants. Home gardeners might be less interested technically, yet soil is the basis of all gardening success. You must accept what is given you, build it up, and keep it built up to a healthful medium for your plants.

Many diseases do not touch garden plants. Often, like

the Chestnut Blight, they are beyond our control. Much is being done to make plants resistant to disease; seeds and bulbs are being treated before being planted, or even sold. We now have rust-resistant Snapdragons and Asters. Some diseases can be prevented by healthful garden practices; such as planting summer Phlox with plenty of compost and good air circulation in order to combat mildew, and by burning old Hollyhock plants and replacing them with new ones to prevent rust. Many diseases occur as a result of too much moisture — high humidity, dampness, or an abundance of rain. In shady gardens, see that your soil is properly drained, give roots as well as stems and leaves plenty of space and air, mulch plants, so that incessant watering during dry spells is not necessary. If foliage is too lush (and apt to rot easily) perhaps you have fed it too much nitrogen and too little potassium.

When spraying is necessary for a disease, try to determine its nature by consulting an expert or a garden encyclopedia (which every gardener should own). For a long time sulphur has been a popular fungicide, but it should not be used in too strong a dose as it burns some foliages and will kill fish in pools by settling on the rocks. Fermate, a new compound, has been satisfactory in combating rust, scab, many leaf-spot diseases, and leaf blights. Fermate at the moment seems to be the best all-around fungicide, and Malathion the best all-around insecticide — if "best" can be applied in either case. Malathion must be used with care, but it is not so posionous as Parathion. Its odor is rather offensive and it should not be applied to fruits and vegetables more than fourteen days before they are harvested.

Whether to use a spray or a dust is usually a matter of opinion. Sprays seem better for eradicating some insects; dusts are usually used for plant diseases. Combinations of both can be either. Some of the powders come in packages that are also dusters; others must be applied with a special machine. Some of the liquid forms need a spreader-sticker, like soap, but explanations on packages of reputable materials should tell you how to use them.

The kind of sprayer is another question; a matter largely of experience and preference. For very small gardens, a good hand-sprayer ($2–$3) will suffice. Efficient gardeners of medium-sized gardens will like the pump type, and small compressed air types, while gardeners of larger acreage will probably prefer wheelbarrow types or knapsacks. Talk with a good hardware or nurseryman before investing in a sprayer. The government Yearbook of Agriculture for 1952, on INSECTS, contains a chart on sprayers as well as much other valuable information.

Rabbits can certainly wreck a garden. They relish the tender new growth of *Dianthus,* Wild Blue Phlox, garden Phlox, Violets, *Euonymous,* Strawberries, *Lychnis, Isatis,* early *Spirea, Artimisia,* fall Asters, Yellow Lady-Slipper, Wild Ginger, *Galax,* and other plants as well as the delicate flower buds of Azaleas, Roses, Laurel, Tulips, and Crocuses. They love the seedlings of Dogwood and *Laburnum,* and they girdle the saplings of almost anything if snow is on the ground and food is scarce; yet they completely ignore carrots and lettuce left out by the owner.

The only real answer is to shoot the rabbits, but there are other ways of changing their habits. They don't like to hop on chicken wire laid flat (so that it won't show) over large patches of rabbit delicacies in late winter. By the time the garden is beginning to look like something, the new growth is tougher and more unpalatable to rabbit lips, and the chicken wire can be removed. Smell of moth balls, tobacco dust, or refuse sprinkled generously around the plants will keep them away, as well as discourage moles, mice, other rodents, and even some dogs.

Woodchucks gobble plants wholesale. Smoke bombs or poison, inserted into one end of their tunnel after the other has been blocked with sod, and shooting, are about the only solutions.

Damage from dogs can be so great to the ornamental garden that additional steps are sometimes necessary. Deterrents which must be used in quantity need replenishing after one or two rains. Shrub guards, with numerous outward-facing wire prongs, are excellent when a number are used to completely discourage the animal. They are practically invisible and can be left in the ground indefinitely. Decorative fences or small pieces of fence can add to the garden's scheme of design as well as acting as a safeguard for a shrub or small garden. In areas which are not prominent low chicken wire fences can protect saplings, newly planted shrubs, or perennials against the ravages of all small animals, at least until the plants are able to withstand such attacks.

Some garden damage is blamed on innocent creatures, many of which are friendly to the garden. Yet the wholesale attempts to eradicate the real pests have resulted in reducing beneficial insects too. We are not only suffering greater infestations of certain pests due to the destruction of their natural parasites but we are destroying large quantities of their casual enemies such as toads, lizards, frogs, snakes, skunks, bats, and birds. The birds do about as efficient an all-around job as any of the insecticides so far employed by man; more efficient in some cases.

Other small creatures also being to nature's "do-gooders" club. Yet not many people professing to love gardens and the out-of-doors will leave a snake to its own devices. Not many welcome bats, frogs, toads, lizards, and skunks as beneficial friends to their gardens.

In many suburban and city gardens there are few friendly creatures left to help eliminate insects. Forget your over-spraying and bid these friends welcome. Plant berried shrubs that the birds can enjoy; provide trees and evergreens for their nests; introduce pools, bird baths, and drinking water for them; put up bird houses; control your cat; feed them when natural food is scarce; allow some of your flowers to go to seed; leave a small part of your yard overgrown and uncared-for, for their security.

There will be something in it for you, too: the bright flashes of color of tanagers, and orioles, and others among the greens, their cheery songs, and their amusing and interesting antics. Somewhere there might be a garden with perfect flowers and uneaten leaves, but would it be perfect with no other life than plants? Wouldn't you miss the nuthatches on the tree-trunks, the yellow goldfinches swaying among blue Bachelors-Buttons, and the friendly voice of the chickadee on a winter's day?

NOTES ON PREYERS

1. Spray your garden early in the season to kill and deter a few insects before they multiply. Let up on spraying later.

2. Try not to spray open flowers from which bees and other insects might gather nectar.

3. Spraying with miscible oils in late winter for scale

insects is preventive. It gets the young as they hatch rather than waiting until damage is done.

4. For canker worm control, use Tanglefoot around trees in the fall. Kill moths before they can crawl up the tree to lay eggs.

5. In late winter pick off tent caterpillar masses. Almost black, about one-half inch long, like a twig enlargment, they can easily be seen. Sometimes more than thirty are found on a single small tree, each of which contains about three hundred eggs. Burn them.

6. To protect Birch trees from the bronze birch borer and beetle keep trees growing vigorously and plant them in shade. Beetles lay their eggs in sunny locations.

7. Rhododendrons, too heavily mulched, invite the pitted ambrosia beetle that feeds (in larval stage) on bark and cambium layer just above the ground. Remove excess mulch, leaving 1–2″, cut infested stem and burn. Dust soil with chlordane.

8. Control of insects often means control of plant diseases.

9. Prolonged dry spells and heat induce greater numbers of spider mites and Japanese beetles the following summer.

10. Hand-picking Japanese beetles and rose chafers is still an important control. Keep a screw-top jar handy, half-filled with water topped with kerosene. Pick off beetles as you walk through the garden. In places of serious infestation use yellow bettle traps. Methoxychlor, DDT, and Malathion kill the beetles but must be used frequently as more grubs emerge from the ground. Chlordane said to control grubs in the ground, but beetles fly in from the outside. The bright spot on the beetle horizon is that a disease is being developed to kill beetle grubs.

11. Comfort yourself with the impossibility of eradicating all insects. There are 680,000 different species named (not counting the 9,000 or so ticks and mites).

12. Discourage stem rot of seedlings by using Vermiculite or other mica products.

13. Eliminate less important host-plants for such things as apple-cedar rust, stone fruit rusts, etc.

14. Use preventive measures when possible.

15. Use plenty of compost to keep plants healthy enough to withstand pests and diseases.

16. Make your own spraying and dusting chart to serve as a reminder.

16

Down to Earth

※✣❀✣❀✣❀✣❀✣❀✣❀✣❀✣❀✣❀✣❀✣❀✣❀✣❀✣❀※

DOWN TO EARTH at last, we come to soil. It is a fascinating subject; intricate, complicated; still a mystery — the unknown world of millions of insects, small animals, protozoa, bacteria, fungi, molds, algae, and other micro-organisms. The large majority of these work for the good of the soil — some bacteria break down dead bodies and waste products into simpler substances that can be used by plants; others grab nitrogen from the air and convert it so that plants can absorb it. The value of earthworms has long been known; their constant tunneling into the soil aerates it.

Soil consists basically of tiny rock particles and organic matter, mixed together and worked on by the elements in such a way as to form good soil or poor soil. When the rock particles are coarse and there is no humus, we have sand. At the other extreme, with particles so fine that the naked eye cannot distinguish them, and there is no humus content, we have clay. In between these two extremes are all sorts of variations, plus the variations made by the basic rocks, the amounts of humus, rainfall, temperature, and climate.

In your garden, you must work with the type of soil already there, building it up with organic matter and other fertilizers, cultivating it to aerate it, turning it over to open it to the elements, constantly improving it to the consistency of a good friable loam — the right amount of sand, clay, and humus, so that when a handful is picked up in a damp condition, it will hold its form before crumbling. Soil that does not cling is too sandy; soil that consolidates easily contains too much clay. Compost improves either kind, by giving body and water-retentive properties to the sandy soil and loosening clay soil so that excess water drains through it.

There is seldom a perfect garden loam. It keeps changing. Your plants themselves change it, by taking out nourishment, by sending down roots, by being turned over to make additional organic matter. Rocks and stones change it, as well as rains, climate and cultivation. In the soil, as well as with plants and flowers, perfection is never achieved.

In the United States many areas have had almost perfect soils. They have become our agricultural districts. Other soils seem poor and deficient. People say they have "run out"; but some claim that the basic elements are still there, and need only organic matter or humus to make the elements available to plant life.

The basic elements needed by both plants and animals are the same: Oxygen, hydrogen, carbon, iron, sulphur, magnesium, calcium, phosphorus, manganese, potassium, copper, boron, iodine, silicon. Of these, the three most important are nitrogen, phosphorus, and potash.

Nitrogen leaches out of the soil most quickly. It is released in the processes of decomposition of organic matter. These processes release nitrogen slowly, but if organic material is being continually replenished, nitrogen is available, if climatic and temperature conditions are right. In cold weather, nitrogen is not released. Therefore, in spring, as the ground is warming up, apply extra nitrogen to boost leaf and stem growth.

INORGANIC NITROGEN: Quick-acting nitrogen, sold as nitrate of soda, ammonium sulphate, and in formula combination as "commercial fertilizer," such as "5-8-7."

ORGANIC NITROGEN: Barnyard manure, cottonseed meal (good for acid-loving plants), dried blood, and blood meal (said to repel night prowlers such as rabbits and deer), bonemeal, and urea, a synthetic organic high in nitrogen currently being used in experimental leaf-feeding.

The chief value of nitrogen is the stimulation of green growth of plants. When there is a deficiency, the leaves turn yellow and finally die. As nitrogen is needed in the decomposition of organic matter, the addition of undecomposed greens like straw, grass clippings, pine needles, etc., may steal the nitrogen from the growing plants. Some people feel this happens in the case of mulching with pine needles (which decompose slowly), or too many fresh grass clippings. The addition of fertilizer containing nitrogen would counteract this tendency, as well as supply the plants with other necessary elements.

Do not add nitrogen in late summer or fall. Leaf growth, apt to be promoted, is likely to freeze and weaken the plant. Manures, however, can be used as a light mulch.

PHOSPHORUS stimulates root growth, is necessary for good blooms and fruits. Lack of it slows down plant growth; often induces red or purplish colors on leaves, particularly the under sides. It is absent, or locked up in compounds in many soils, notably those in New England. Compost and humus in the soil tend to release locked-up phosphorus, but slowly.

For quick release use phosphate rock, superphosphate (phosphate rock ground and treated with sulphuric acid), or cottonseed meal (7 percent nitrogen, 3 percent phosphorus, 2 percent potash). Bonemeal is an excellent organic source of phosphorus, but works slowly (six months to three years to be used by the plant). Good to turn into ground in autumn for availability in the spring. Tends to sweeten the soil; do not use around acid-demanding plants.

POTASSIUM OR POTASH is necessary for good root growth. Enables plants to withstand disease; strengthens stems and leaf growth; improves flowers. One of the best sources of potash is wood ashes which can be scattered in late winter and carried down to the roots by spring rains. Muriate of potash and sulphate of potash (both inorganic), and potash in formula can be used, but all contain some lime and must not be used around acid-demanding plants.

These three oft-mentioned elements leach out of the soil, or are generally less available in certain soils, so that they must be replenished. Other elements, usually referred to as "trace elements," are present in most soils.

Their availability to plants is a different matter, however. The best way of making them available is by the incorporation of organic material into the soil — such materials as animal residue (manures, ground bones, dried blood), and partially decomposed vegetable matter (leaves, grass clippings, pea pods and other vegetable refuse, weeds). Favorable temperature and moisture conditions are necessary too.

Decomposing organic matter in the soil frees mineral elements so that plants can use them, and helps retain moisture in the soil. Nutrients can be absorbed by roots only in solution or when there is sufficient moisture. The millions of micro-organisms, already at work on decomposing matter, are stimulated to greater activity. They join forces with bacteria, fungi, molds, etc., already in the soil to break down organic substances into materials the plants can use. This process goes on continually — doing the greatest good at the height of greatest activity — until all matter is thoroughly decomposed and the soil is inert.

As plants cannot live in an inert soil, organic matter must be *supplied constantly* to keep the soil a going concern. It is like a huge factory containing millions of smaller factories. For raw materials there are the basic elements, animal and plant residue, and soil particles. The workers are plant roots, air, water, weather, temperature, and millions of micro-organisms, all working to manufacture ideal conditions for growing plants. The smaller factories are the plants themselves. They take their raw materials from the soil, air, and sun, and manufacture their own food. When raw materials are exhausted, more must be added to keep the factories going.

In spring, before the weather has become warm enough so the soil factory is well under way, give non-acid-loving plants a boost with a little quickly available fertilizer. The formula fertilizers are easiest to use. They are usually called "commercial fertilizers," and come in large bags of granulated pinkish or white substance sold as "5-8-7," "5-10-5," etc. The first number is the percentage of nitrogen the bag contains; the second number, the phosphorus; and the third, the potash. Work in 1–2 tablespoons around plants at intervals of two to four weeks before they bloom. Broadcast, it is spread at the ratio of 1 pound per 25 square feet. Do not use much on annuals; they prefer a moderately rich soil containing plenty of humus.

With nutrients so easily available in such aggregates,

why should this kind of fertilizer not be depended on wholly for feeding the garden, instead of other fertilizing materials which have to go through elaborate changes before the plants can use them? Like vitamin tablets, so-called commercial fertilizers are quick acting. They are fine for supplementary feedings, but they can never take the place of organic materials, which condition the soil as well as adding nutrients and making other nutrients available. A hard soil fed only with inorganc nutrients soon becomes unworkable. A good soil fed only with inorganic nutrients soon becomes hard.

Compost and barnyard manure are good for all kinds of soil. They are natural soil-conditioners. They lighten and aerate hard clayey soil, making it more porous so that water does not remain in it to drown the plants. They give body to a light, sandy soil, make it more water-retentive, and a better working medium for plants. The ideal plant soil is one that is neither too clayey, or too sandy, that contains plenty of organic material, that holds its shape when a moist handful is squeezed, but crumbles as it is cultivated. A good soil is a friable loam.

ANIMAL MANURES are excellent when animals have been bedded down with straw or peat moss, which help retain valuable nitrogen source-urea. Any barnyard manure is good, but it should be four to six months old when used. Fresh manure or inorganic fertilizer burns if it comes in contact with a plant's roots, leaves, or stem. It is best to turn fresh manure into a soil several weeks or months before you plant.

Chicken and sheep manures, more caustic, must be used with care. Best to mix any manure well into the soil and keep it away from plants. Less efficient, but good, are packaged fertilizers with an organic base, such as Bovung, Driconure, Malorganite (from sewage plants).

Green manure is excellent for a starter in building up very poor soil. It is a green cover crop planted and turned into the soil while still tender, adding nutrients as it undergoes decomposition. The best Cover Crops are any of the legumes (Clover, Alfalfa, Soy Beans, etc.) or Rye, which is often planted in the fall and turned under in spring.

COMPOST is the result of saving all kinds of organic materials, mixing them together where they receive warmth, air, and moisture, and allowing time (nine to eighteen months) to do the rest. To a beginning gardener with soil so poor that it will not support perennials, and who turns to composted materials in despair, the results are no less than miraculous. But an abundance must be used, and used before is has become thoroughly decomposed.

Recipe for a COMPOST PILE: One layer of sod turned grass down; one layer each of dried leaves, soil, manure, grass clippings, vegetable refuse, soil; and back to sod again, with other layers repeated. Spread layers evenly onto a pile and leave a depression in the top to catch and hold extra water. Turn over and remake every few weeks. Keep at least two of these piles going, one to use this year, one to use next year.

But compost piles takes time and energy. Adding organic materials as you acquire them, in a pit in the ground, is easier on the back, and is less apt to be unsightly. It is wise, however, to hide any compost pile behind evergreens or small trees.

The why of a compost pile is good to know. Any organic matter must have warmth, moisture, and air in order to decompose. Bacteria and other micro-organisms are stimulated to greatest activity during warm weather. Make the most of this, and start your compost pile in the spring with the leaves you rake from your yard. Add grass clippings and weeds as you acquire them. Throw on soil, good or bad, and some manure if you have it. Kitchen refuse is good too, particularly pea pods, which supply the nitrogen-grabbing bacteria. Alternate layers of leaves and green material with a scattering of soil. Materials will decompose faster. Grass clippings usually take only a few months to decompose; weeds with roots not much longer. Oak leaves need about two years; tougher leaves take longer. Anything tougher than that (flower stalks, sawdust, wood chips, etc.) should not be added to the regular compost. Mixed all together, the compost will be in various stages of decomposition which is good.

MOISTURE is necessary to microbe activity. Therefore, choose your compost site in the shade, where it will not dry out too quickly, and turn the hose on it during dry spells.

Air does its part. People worry that compost piles in the earth do not get enough air. Leave part of the pit empty, and air will get to it. Turning the compost exposes hidden parts to the air, and enables the compost to decompose evenly. If all parts are not systematically exposed, dry leaves will be found intact months, even years, later.

LIME AND COMMERCIAL FERTILIZERS or new activators can be added to compost to supply further stimulation. They will add nutrients and destroy odors. Lime, however, should not be added to compost to be used around acid-loving plants. I make compost without lime, and add it only around those plants that require it, and I use wood ashes instead of lime.

LIME performs a necessary function when needed, and is sold as quick-acting, hydrated lime, and crushed limestone, which is slower-acting and less apt to burn plants. It improves the physical condition of many soils, coagulates fine clay particles, and stimulates bacterial activity. It contains calcium and magnesium and releases other nutrients and neutralizes an acid soil.

The acidity or alkalinity of soils is hard to describe. Besides being good or poor, soil has what is known as a pH count, a measuring unit for the hydrogen ion concentration. The scale runs from 0 to 14, with 7 being neutral. Soils with a count below 7 are acid; those above 7 are alkaline.

Most plants don't care about the pH count, as long as there is food and organic matter. A few plants must have an alkaline soil, or a neutral soil (notably, many vegetables, Monkshood, the Hop-Tree, and a number of sun-loving plants). A great many plants must have acid conditions and do not thrive on a pH count of more than 6 (usually 4–6). The most notable of these belong to the Heath family: Laurel, Rhododendrons, Azaleas, Andromeda, *Leucothoe*, Blueberry, Bearberry, Trailing Arbutus, Wintergreen, and others. Most of the Heath family like semi-shade, protection from wind, acid soil, and an abundance of humus in the soil. Almost all broad-leaved evergreens like an acid soil. Needled evergreens usually grow in an acid soil, contribute toward making a soil acid, but will tolerate nearly neutral conditions. Many spring wild flowers must have an acid soil.

Soils in different areas of the country — and even within a state, or a town — can be notably acid or alkaline. Usually this condition is due to the underlying rock formation. Granites, mica, sandstone, promote acid soils; and the soils containing limestone, marble, and other rocks are also likely to be alkaline.

If you have oaks and evergreen trees growing naturally on your property, or in a nearby area, the chances are your soil is acid. If there are maples and beeches, your soil is probably neutral or alkaline. Have your soil tested at a government agricultural station or school, or test it yourself with litmus paper, or a soil-testing kit.

Buy red and blue litmus paper at a drugstore; place a slip of each in a muddy slit in the ground. If the red paper turns blue, the soil is alkaline; if the blue paper turns red, the soil is acid. A neutral condition is indicated by either paper turning purple. *Hydrangea macrophylla* is also a good indicator of soil acidity. If it produces blue flowers, the soil is acid; if the blossoms are pink, the soil is alkaline; purplish flowers indicate a neutral soil.

Soil-testing kits undoubtedly have their place in the hands of the chemically-minded gardener, but litmus paper is exact enough for the small gardener, inasmuch as the demands of most of the acid-lovers fluctuate between a pH count of 4–6.5. In testing for deficiency of nitrogen, phosphorus, potash, etc., how does the amateur know how much of the chemical to add, with plants varying in sizes and demands? It is almost impossible to satisfy the specific requirements of so many plants crowded side by side in the flower garden. Furthermore, adding one element, without knowledge, can upset the balance of a whole area.

This delicate balance of soil properties is not entirely understood. An overdose of a certain element may change the entire chemical structure of a soil. Even compost changes the chemical structure, but does it in a natural way, aerating it and promoting the right kind of bacterial activity. Lime unlocks too many nutrients for some plants, while "locking up" iron. Experts wonder if the reason acid-loving plants do not respond to lime is that they do not like what it does to a soil.

Many shade-loving plants are also acid-loving. If you have a naturally acid soil and keep it plentifully supplied with compost made principally from oak leaves, it will remain in good condition for most of your plants. If your soil tends toward alkalinity, and you want to grow acid-loving plants, add oak-leaf compost if you can get it. Peat moss is a fair substitute, both as a soil-conditioner and a mulch. Many nurseries depend entirely on peat moss in planting acid-demanding plants. You can make an acid compost by adding "1 cup of either ammonium sulphate or nitrate, plus 1½ cup of 20% superphosphate and 1 tablespoon magnesium sulphate (epsom salts) to each well-packed bushel of material" (H. Gleason Mattoon, *Horticultural Newsletter,* July 19, 1954).

If your soil, as well as that of the surrounding country-side, is definitely alkaline, you will have difficulty growing many acid-loving plants. In parts of Florida people cannot grow Azaleas because of underground alkaline springs, while gardens within ten miles support beautiful Azaleas. Perhaps the easiest thing in the long run is to plant Oak trees, and depend on their leaves and on peat moss; and to fertilize (until the Oak leaves are a regular thing) with superphosphate and cottonseed meal. Water with left-over tea and scatter used tea leaves around the base of acid-loving plants. Tea contains tannic acid which the plants like.

If you are a gardener-in-the-shade, compost of your own making is the best soil-conditioner you can have. Most commercial soil-conditioners are meant for only a hard soil; compost is not only good for a heavy, clayey soil, and hard sub-soil, but for a sandy soil as well.

When you transplant or divide perennials or work around Laurels, Azaleas, and other shrubs, have on hand a bushel of compost, made principally from oak leaves. Use it generously. Try to add some to the soil around every plant, every year. Mulch with peat moss or pine needles. The praises of composting and mulching can be sung only by those who have tried them.

17

Plants and More Plants

Next to the satisfaction of the beginner who finds his plants actually growing, comes the thrill of propagating his plants; not only from seeds — though that is fun too — but from making cuttings, and making new plants by layering.

For years people who have not claimed to be gardeners have grown house plants from "slips." Their knowledge of "slipping" is passed along from one house plant enthusiast to another, with hints such as "This plant roots better in water," but "That plant doesn't mind being set right in the soil."

It is a miracle to me that one has only to take the end of a branch, stick it in the ground and treat it properly, to have it grow. A cutting or slip is nothing more than the tip end of a branch, 4-10 inches long, depending upon the plant. Usually a cutting is taken from the current year's growth, after it has become firm enough to snap when bent. But again, that depends on the individual plant and your own experience. Your experience is gained by trying different cuttings

261

to find out which roots easily and which doesn't, how long it takes, and what to do about it.

The theory of rooting cuttings out-of-doors, or in a greenhouse, is exactly the same as that of raising plants from slips. Roots, properly induced, spring from the broken end of a branch, or from places which naturally give rise to plant growth; notably, the nodes. A node is a place along the stem from which a leaf or flower bud grows. Consequently, one or two nodes should be buried in the rooting medium to give the cutting as much chance as possible to root.

The rooting medium can be sand, peat moss, Vermiculite, soil, even water, or a mixture of some of these. It depends on the preference of the gardener. Sand is probably the most popular medium. Sandy soil that is about half peat moss or leaf mould makes a fluffy medium that does not pack too tightly, yet it has food value in case the cutting is not transplanted as soon as it has rooted. Once rooted, a cutting must have nourishment or it dies. Sand and Vermiculite have no food value; peat moss has little, although you can root cuttings in all of these.

A cutting needs warmth, moisture, air, and protection from the sun in order to grow roots. An evergreen cutting, which gives off moisture through its leaves, should have added moisture or humidity. A small glass jar, or a polyethylene bag can supply this humidity for the amateur. Greenhouses, and specially prepared propagating houses are used by the professional.

The moisture in the rooting medium should never be excessive. Why Begonias, African Violets, and other plants root readily in water, yet rot if they stand in damp sand or soil, is a mystery; but it's a fact and must be guarded against. So have the rooting medium moist, but not wet. It is not difficult, for you have only to try a few to pick up the knack of knowing when the rooting medium is in the right condition.

To get the "feel" of rooting cuttings, make one; make several. Start with a slip from a houseplant indoors during the winter. Take a large flower pot, 8–10 inches in diameter, place a layer of stones, or broken crockery at the bottom for drainage, and build up with a little soil. In the center, but so that the tops are even, set a smaller pot, 2–3 inches in diameter, which has had the drainage hole closed up. To do this, place a stone over the hole and pour hot paraffin in to seal it tightly. Fill the space between the two pots with fluffy, humusy soil (one-half sandy loam, one-half peat moss or leaf-mold sifted together). This soil preparation should be soft and fluffy to the touch and have good drainage (so that water poured on it will drain away almost immediately and not stand on top).

With sharp scissors or pruning shears, snip off several inches of firm new growth from a house plant like Coleus, Patience Plant, Begonia; or take a cutting from an outdoor shrub like *Taxus*, Oleander, Azalea, or Laurel. Peel off lower leaves of cuttings, leaving 1–2 inches of bare stem to go below ground and several inches for above the ground. With a knife make an incision into the soil, set in the cutting, and carefully close the soil around it. Place cuttings about two inches apart, so they won't touch each other. If needed, place a small jelly tumbler over each. Keep the small pot in the center filled with water. Depending upon the humidity of the house, this will need filling once or maybe twice a day. Enough moisture is eased through the walls of the smaller pot to keep the soil in the larger pot at the correct degree of dampness to root most cuttings.

House plants, such as those mentioned above, and other easily-rooted plants, probably will not need added humidity. But if the cutting starts looking wilted, place a small jar over it, and watch carefully during the next few days that this does not keep the cutting too wet. For the first few days the cutting should remain pert and green. Later, it might drop its leaves, but it will grow more if it roots.

Evergreens and some plants (Marguerites, Roses, etc.,) need all the top moisture they can get and will welcome a glass covering. Some cuttings, like some plants, will not thrive in the dry atmosphere of most homes. If they are rooted indoors, plant them outside as soon as possible, or keep them covered until they can be set out-of-doors. Some cuttings like a covering for a few days or weeks only. If you suspect they are rooting, remove the jar for a few hours at a time. If the plant wilts, replace the jar immediately; if not, keep it off for a little longer, and work up to leaving the jar off altogether.

This probably sounds like a lot of trouble, but once you gain the knack of it, it will prove a fascinating hobby. Keep your cuttings-pot near at hand; beside the kitchen sink, in the dining room, or breakfast nook, where you can see it frequently. Try easy things first; then others; try a number of them. Not all will root, even if conditions are ideal, but when your first cuttings begin to "strike" you will want to make more.

Another way of rooting cuttings in the house is to place a single cutting in a small flower pot filled with fluffy soil. Water, to make soil of even moistness, and enclose the whole thing in an air-tight polyethylene bag — the same kind that is used to wrap up food for freezer-storage. Bags can be bought at a freezer-supply store, made from plastics by the yard, or saved from nut bread or other food that comes in air-tight bags (not vegetable bags, that are usually full of holes).

Again, the secret of this method of rooting a cutting is the correct degree of moisture in the rooting medium. It must be damp but cannot be wet.

Perhaps you would prefer to learn to make cuttings out-of-doors. As shade is almost as essential as the proper degree of moisture, choose for your "cuttings garden" a spot under a tree or shrub that is accessible to you and the water supply. See that the soil in this area is free from stones and roots and has good drainage. It should be a sandy loam with a quantity of leafmold or peat moss mixed with it, but it does not have to be sifted.

Every plant has its own characteristic way of growing and developing roots on cuttings taken from it. Some root more easily, or just as easily in water (Pussy Willow, Forsythia, Ivy, etc.). Others must be taken at exactly the right time during the growing period (*Artemisia* var. Silver Mound — in early spring); others (particularly evergreens) must have the current year's growth at just the right degree of firmness — when it breaks with a snap when bent. A general rule to follow is to make cuttings from most perennials in early spring when they are beginning to grow, and from evergreens and shrubs in early summer when new growth has hardened. But TRY anything at ANY time.

There are a number of so-called hormone powders on the market — Rootone, Root-prod, etc. These stimulate root growth and are supposed to shorten the time it takes to grow roots. Some people have found them invaluable and they are well worth trying, particularly in air-layering. But people have been propagating plants from cuttings for hundreds of years without the aid of additional chemicals.

Although the current year's growth of evergreens are easiest to root, I have often taken cuttings of *Ilex crenata, Taxus,* Boxwood and others quite early in the spring before the new growth has fully developed. Then the previous year's growth must be relied on. Take a cutting anywhere from 6–10 inches long from a healthy looking branch. Peel off lower leaves for about one and one-half inches. Dust stem and end lightly with a hormone powder and insert 1–2 inches gently into the ground as described above. Cover with a glass jar taller than the cutting. See that the soil is continually kept moist. Mulching will help do this. In the case of large-leaved evergreens, trim the leaves left on the cutting to about one-half their original length or less. This is to decrease loss of moisture through evaporation and to make the cuttings less awkward. Trim off flower buds and flower growth.

Rose cuttings should be long enough to bury two nodes and leave 2–3 sets of leaves above the ground. Remove any flower bud so that the strength can go to the making of roots. Cover with tall glass jar. Cuttings of deciduous shrubs and trees can be made in the same way. Sometimes the leaves drop off, but don't abandon the hope of the cuttings taking root; this often happens and new leaves will usually grow, which tell you that your cutting has "struck."

It doesn't hurt a cutting to remove the jar once in a while as long as you don't disturb the cutting. In fact, it is a good thing to let in some air. Watch for signs of its being too wet or too dry, but don't leave the jar off entirely until the cutting has rooted. Then, don't be in a hurry to move the newly-rooted plants. Leave Rose and evergreen cuttings alone over the first winter. If they are moved in the fall, even though they have grown a substantial cluster of roots, severe cold or the heaving and thawing of the ground may kill them.

Many times the easiest way to make new plants is to chop apart the old ones, or take sucker growths from the sides of the large plants. Most of us are familiar with Lilac suckers. Not all of us are familiar with the sucker growths of Japanese Quince, Azalea, Deutzia, Flowering Almond, Sweet Pepper-Bush, Witch-Hazel, and a host of other deciduous shrubs. The new growth of some evergreens springs from the root system too, notably *Leucothoe*, Mountain Andromeda, young Laurel plants, etc.

All these so-called suckers are potential shrubs. One has only to chop them away from the parent-shrub, with as much root as possible, establish them in good hur `sy soil, keep watered during droughts, and one has a new plant. This is best done in early spring, just before, or at the beginning of, the active growing season, when nature gives natural impetus to growing things.

Layering is another interesting way of propagating plants. It is probably the easiest way in which roots are induced by man, for a layering can be made and forgotten until the branch has grown enough roots to be severed from the parent-shrub. It does not even have to be watered, although it helps to supplement natural moisture.

Choose a branch that grows naturally close to the ground and bend it down. Where it touches the earth (1–3′ from the tip) scrape off a little of the bark through to the cambium layer, the inner growing tissue just under the bark. Touch the scraped place with a hormone power if you have some, heap humusy soil up under and over it and weight it down with a rock heavy enough to keep the scraped place buried.

In the North it takes about two years for a ground-layering to grow roots so that it can be cut from the parent and transplanted. Many shrubs layer themselves when a branch touches the soil. All such layerings should be transplanted as early in the spring as the ground can be worked. They must be kept well-watered during dry spells.

Air-layering, or "mossing off," as it is called in the South, where it is practiced by many amateurs, is an ancient Chinese method of propagating plants. A ball of moist sphagnum moss was fastened around a portion of a branch in the air, where a little bark had been scraped off. This had to be kept moist continually until roots had grown from the scraped place — sometimes a matter of months, a feat which called for many ingenious devices. Today however, with new plastics to keep the layerings air-tight, it is comparatively easy. And there is a thrill of accomplishment when the method succeeds.

The theory is much the same as that of other layering except that it is done in the air. A branch 1–3′ long is chosen in the North, but in the South, where weather and humidity are so conducive to plant growth, branches up to 5–6′ are air-layered with remarkable success.

From the end of a branch, 1–3′, scrape off the bark in a ring not quite all around the branch. Touch the wound with hormone powder and cover with moist (not wet) sphagnum moss about the size of a baseball. Around this wrap a piece of polyethylene plastic, about 12″ square. Secure firmly at top and bottom with electrician's tape or waxed crepe paper — the kind used for corsages. Be sure that the plastic is overlapped on the *under* side of the branch so that rain won't seep in.

In two to three months, try to determine through the plastic covering whether the branch has grown roots. You might have to undo one end. If a layering hasn't "struck" by fall, let it go through the winter. When rooted, cut the branch above the layering and remove plastic. Leave moss on when planting. Set into the ground so that soil comes well up over rooted section. Treat like any rooted cutting, planting it out of the wind and weighting the base with stones.

There are other ways of propagating plants asexually — budding, grafting, etc. — but these are more difficult and usually require more space and facilities than most of us have. However, if you are interested, there are books on the subject, sections in garden encyclopedias, and articles. Who knows? You might find propagating plants so fascinating that you'll want to go in for it in a big way! Then you'll have to have a plant nursery.

This too, should be in the shade, in good (but not rich) friable loam. For acid-loving plants incorporate plenty of Oak leafmold. For others, rake in a little bone meal. Fence the place in against children's eager feet, grown-ups' clumsy ones, and "predatory beasts." The nursery should be accessible to water, for the roots of young plants should be kept fairly moist until they have grown deep into the soil. Mulch the plants to keep down the weeds and keep in the moisture. When they are sturdy and large enough, move them to their permanent homes.

We have discussed at length a few of the ways of increasing plants asexually — by growing a new plant from a piece of the parent-plant. This is the only way of reproducing a plant exactly. On the other hand, sexual reproduction (by seeds, so-called because the flowers must be fertilized through the union of the two sexes, before the seed can ripen) might or might not give us the plant we want. Plants raised from seeds are usually so similar that the casual eye can detect no differences, yet they are apt to be different. By weeding out poor specimens, and developing desirable characteristics, hybridizers have produced some of our rare and lovely flowers of today.

Naturally when we purchase seeds from reputable seed houses, we expect to raise the plants we read about in the catalogues. But if we were to plant the seeds of our seedlings (even though we gave them as much care as we had given the original seeds) we would be disappointed more often than not, because most of those seedlings would revert to characteristics of past generations.

We still, however, grow many annuals, trees, shrubs, and perennials in their original forms. And seeds of wild flowers come relatively true to type, though there is always the possibility of variation. It is this possibility that has suggested improvement of some of the species, and offers a challenge to the adventurous gardener.

The requirements for seed germination are the same as they are for making cuttings—warmth, moisture, time, and a porous germinating medium. As for cuttings, the germinating medium can be sand, peat moss, vermiculite, or soil. Although there is enough food in each seed to grow the first set of true leaves, it is easy to forget seedlings once they have germinated in a sterile substance; and before you know it, you've lost them. Use a soil mixture similar to that for cuttings—one-half good sandy loam, one-half rotted leafmold, or compost sifted through a fine screen.

A good seed-planting container is a coffee can with three holes punched ½–1″ from the bottom (for drainage), and the bottom lined with stones before the soil mixture is added. Coffee cans are light and easily handled; they are deep, and a small piece of glass readily fits over them. Also use the pot-within-pot method, or a flat. The secret of growing plants from seeds, as well as from cuttings, is the degree of moisture in soil and air. Too much water means too little oxygen, which is as essential to plants as to human beings. Giving your seed-container the neck-bath treatment (setting seed-flat or can in water up to its neck and letting it absorb moisture that way) gives uniformity without drowning the plants. Additional directions for planting seeds are given in Chapter 5.

Just as some cuttings root in a few weeks, and others take months, some types of seeds are rabbits and tortoises in germinating. Often the length of time is indicated on a seed-package, and occasionally germinating tables will be found in catalogues or articles. When the seeds are up, polyethylene bags can become individual greenhouses. Arrange them like tents over the containers. Bring seedlings gradually into the light and—when they are established with a good-root system, transplant to a coldframe or to their permanent homes. Young perennials or biennials are usually classed as "tender" for their first winter, and are best kept in a coldframe until the following March to May. If you have no coldframe, try the cellar or a cool pantry (45°). Keep them in a semi-dormant state, watering every few weeks, or when they look dry. Plants do not grow much in a cold atmosphere, consequently cannot use much water. Understanding this, people would be surprised at the number of tender plants they could nurse through the winter in a cool closet, cellar, or attic. But once inoculated with plant-growing fever you'll find a coldframe a necessity for this and many other things for which it can be used.

There are many ways of making a coldframe, but this one is easy even for a person with little mechanical ability.

At a junk yard buy two old 3' x 3' window sashes (about $1.00 apiece). Build the coldframe itself out of two layers of cinder blocks, laid out in a rectangle approximately 6′ x 3′ to fit under the window sashes. Dig the whole into the ground, rather than let it rest on top.

Some of the many invaluable uses of the coldframe are:

1. In spring, for the sowing of early annuals.

2. In spring, for raising early lettuce and radishes.

3. In summer, for the planting of perennials and biennials.

4. For making cuttings.

5. For keeping rooted cuttings and tender young seedlings.

6. In autumn, setting in rooted cuttings, seedlings, etc., for winter keeping.

7. Keeping potted Tulips, Daffodils for indoor forcing.

8. For heeling in Chrysanthemums and other tender perennials for the winter.

Index

273